UNDERSTANDING DRUGS

Cocaine and Crack

TITLES IN THE *UNDERSTANDING DRUGS* SERIES

UNDERSTANDING DRUGS

Cocaine and Crack

ALAN HECHT, D.C.

CONSULTING EDITOR
DAVID J. TRIGGLE, PH.D.
University Professor
School of Pharmacy and Pharmaceutical Sciences
State University of New York at Buffalo

CHELSEA HOUSE
An Infobase Learning Company

Chelsea House
An imprint of Infobase Learning
132 West 31st Street
New York NY 10001

Library of Congress Cataloging-in-Publication Data

Hecht, Alan.
    Cocaine and crack / Alan Hecht ; consulting editor David J. Triggle.
        p. cm. — (Understanding drugs)
    Includes bibliographical references and index.
    ISBN-13: 978-1-60413-536-7 (alk. paper)
    ISBN-10: 1-60413-536-0 (alk. paper)   1. Cocaine—History.   2. Crack (Drug)—
        History.   I. Triggle, D. J.   II. Title.
    HV5810.H43   2011
    362.29'8—dc22   2010046555

Chelsea House books are available at special discounts when purchased in bulk quantities for businesses, associations, institutions, or sales promotions. Please call our Special Sales Department in New York at (212) 967-8800 or (800) 322-8755.

You can find Chelsea House on the World Wide Web at
http://www.infobaselearning.com

Text design by Kerry Casey
Cover design by Alicia Post
Composition by Newgen
Cover printed by Yurchak Printing, Landisville, Pa.
Book printed and bound by Yurchak Printing, Landisville, Pa.
Date printed: April 2011
Printed in the United States of America

10 9 8 7 6 5 4 3 2 1

This book is printed on acid-free paper.

All links and Web addresses were checked and verified to be correct at the time of publication. Because of the dynamic nature of the Web, some addresses and links may have changed since publication and may no longer be valid.

Contents

foreword

THE USE AND ABUSE OF DRUGS

For thousands of years, humans have used a variety of sources with which to cure their ills, cast out devils, promote their well-being, relieve their misery, and control their fertility. Until the beginning of the twentieth century, the agents used were all of natural origin, including many derived from plants as well as elements such as antimony, sulfur, mercury, and arsenic. The sixteenth-century alchemist and physician Paracelsus used mercury and arsenic in his treatment of syphilis, worms, and other diseases that were common at that time; his cure rates, however, remain unknown. Many drugs used today have their origins in natural products. Antimony derivatives, for example, are used in the treatment of the nasty tropical disease leishmaniasis. These plant-derived products represent molecules that have been "forged in the crucible of evolution" and continue to supply the scientist with molecular scaffolds for new drug development.

Our story of modern drug discovery may be considered to start with the German physician and scientist Paul Ehrlich, often called the father of chemotherapy. Born in 1854, Ehrlich became interested in the ways in which synthetic dyes, then becoming a major product of the German fine chemical industry, could selectively stain certain tissues and components of cells. He reasoned that such dyes might form the basis for drugs that could interact selectively with diseased or foreign cells and organisms. One of Ehrlich's early successes was development of the arsenical "606"—patented under the name *Salvarsan*—as a treatment for syphilis. Ehrlich's goal was to create a "magic bullet," a drug that would target only the diseased cell or the invading disease-causing organism and have no effect on healthy cells and tissues. In this he was not successful, but his great research did lay the groundwork for the successes of the twentieth century, including the discovery of the sulfonamides and the antibiotic penicillin. The latter agent saved countless lives during World War II. Ehrlich, like many scientists, was an optimist. On the eve of World War I, he wrote, "Now that the liability to, and danger of, disease are to a large extent circumscribed—the efforts of chemotherapeutics are directed as far as possible to fill up the gaps left in this ring." As we shall see in the pages of this volume, it is neither the first nor the last time that science has proclaimed its victory over nature, only to have to see this optimism dashed in the light of some freshly emerging infection.

From these advances, however, has come the vast array of drugs that are available to the modern physician. We are increasingly close to Ehrlich's magic bullet: Drugs can now target very specific molecular defects in a number of cancers, and doctors today have the ability to investigate the human genome to more effectively match the drug and the patient. In the next one to two decades, it is almost certain that the cost of "reading" an individual genome will be sufficiently cheap that, at least in the developed world, such personalized medicines will become the norm. The development of such drugs, however, is extremely costly and raises significant social issues, including equity in the delivery of medical treatment.

The twenty-first century will continue to produce major advances in medicines and medicine delivery. Nature is, however, a resilient foe. Diseases and organisms develop resistance to existing drugs, and new drugs must constantly be developed. (This is particularly true for anti-infective and anticancer agents.) Additionally, new and more lethal forms of existing infectious diseases can develop rapidly. With the ease of global travel, these can spread from Timbuktu to Toledo in less than 24 hours and become pandemics. Hence the current concerns with avian flu. Also, diseases that have previously been dormant or geographically circumscribed may suddenly break out worldwide. (Imagine, for example, a worldwide pandemic of Ebola disease, with public health agencies totally overwhelmed.) Finally, there are serious concerns regarding the possibility of man-made epidemics occurring through the deliberate or accidental spread of disease agents—including manufactured agents, such as smallpox with enhanced lethality. It is therefore imperative that the search for new medicines continue.

All of us at some time in our life will take a medicine, even if it is only aspirin for a headache or to reduce cosmetic defects. For some individuals, drug use will be constant throughout life. As we age, we will likely be exposed to a variety of medications—from childhood vaccines to drugs to relieve pain caused by a terminal disease. It is not easy to get accurate and understandable information about the drugs that we consume to treat diseases and disorders. There are, of course, highly specialized volumes aimed at medical or scientific professionals. These, however, demand a sophisticated knowledge base and experience to be comprehended. Advertising on television is widely available but provides only fleeting information, usually about only a single drug and designed to market rather than inform. The intent of this series of books, **Understanding Drugs**, is to provide the lay reader with intelligent, readable, and accurate descriptions of drugs, why and how they are used, their limitations, their side effects, and their future. The series will discuss both *"treatment drugs"*—typically, but not exclusively, prescription drugs, that have well-established criteria of both efficacy and safety—and *"drugs of abuse,"* agents that have pronounced pharmacological and physiological effects but that are, for a variety of reasons, not to be considered for therapeutic purposes. It is our hope that these books will provide readers with sufficient information to satisfy their immediate needs and to serve as an adequate base for further investigation and for asking intelligent questions of health care providers.

—David J. Triggle, Ph.D.
University Professor
School of Pharmacy and Pharmaceutical Sciences
State University of New York at Buffalo

1

What Are Cocaine and Crack?

In his sophomore year of high school, Artie went to a party where, it turned out, no parents were at home. His host was a schoolmate who had a reputation for not following the rules very often. He introduced Artie to cocaine. At first, Artie was reluctant. He had heard that there might be some adverse effects. He was concerned about the police raiding the house. And he didn't want his father to ever find out. Nevertheless, he gave in and snorted some cocaine.

Almost immediately, Artie experienced a strong feeling of confidence, alertness, and wakefulness. He had never felt this way before. It seemed that negative feelings didn't matter anymore. He was a new person and wanted to continue feeling this way all of the time.

COCAINE

Cocaine (**benzoylmethylecgonine**) is derived from the leaves of the **coca plant** (*Erythoxylum coca*), native to the northwestern area of South America. Grown predominantly in Bolivia and Peru, it is also found in Africa and Australia. The plant has been used by indigenous people of the Andean region for centuries. The leaves are chewed in order to increase stamina, decrease hunger, improve functioning at high altitudes, and relieve nausea. Cocaine is produced by making a crude paste from the coca leaves, which is then subject to further purification steps.

Figure 1.1   Bolivian coca (*Erythroxylon coca, Erythroxylum coca*) plant, the leaves of which are used to make cocaine.   *(©blickwinkel / Alamy)*

Cocaine is a powerfully addictive **central nervous system** stimulant that is smoked, injected, rubbed into the gums, or, more commonly, snorted. It is referred to by many street names including coke, snow, flake, blow, and dozens of other terms depending on the form in which it is used and in reference to the condition of the user.

According to the National Survey on Drug Use and Health (NSDUH), in 2007 there were 2.1 million current (past-month) cocaine users, of which approximately 610,000 were current **crack** users. Adults aged 18 to 25 years had a higher rate of current cocaine use than any other age group, with 1.7 percent of young adults reporting past month cocaine use. Overall, men reported higher rates of current cocaine use than women. Ethnic and racial differences also occur, with the highest rates in those reporting two or more races (1.1 percent), followed by Hispanics (1.0 percent), whites (0.9 percent), and African-Americans (0.8 percent).[1] In addition, nearly 1.6 million Americans met *Diagnostic and Statistical Manual of Mental Disorders* criteria for dependence or abuse of cocaine (in any form) in the past 12 months.

COMMON STREET TERMS
ASSOCIATED WITH COCAINE

Street Term	Definition
all-American drug	cocaine
base	cocaine; crack
big C	cocaine
black rock	crack cocaine
blow	cocaine; to inhale cocaine; to smoke marijuana; to inject heroin
break night	to stay up all night, until daybreak, on a cocaine binge
coke bar	a bar where cocaine is openly used
do a line	to inhale cocaine
dream	cocaine
flake	cocaine
freebase	to smoke cocaine; or, crack cocaine itself
geek-joints	cigarettes or cigars filled with tobacco and crack; a marijuana cigarette laced with crack or powdered cocaine
happy dust	cocaine
macaroni and cheese	$5 pack of marijuana and a dime bag of cocaine
nose candy	cocaine
Peruvian flake	cocaine
rock star	female who trades sex for crack or money to buy crack; a person who uses rock cocaine
snort	to inhale cocaine or other powder drug; to use an inhalant; or, powder cocaine
spaceball	PCP used with crack or powder cocaine
speedball	cocaine mixed with heroin; crack and heroin smoked together; methylphenidate (Ritalin) mixed with heroin; amphetamine

Source: Office of National Drug Control Policy, "Street Terms: Drugs and the Drug Trade. Drug Type: Cocaine," http://www.whitehousedrugpolicy.gov/streetterms/ByType.asp?intTypeID=3, (accessed March 22, 2010).

Figure 1.2 Cocaine is a powerfully addictive stimulant drug. *(U.S. Drug Enforcement Administration)*

In the 1880s cocaine became popular among medical professionals as a local anesthetic used in surgeries of the throat, nose, and eye. Not only did it block pain, but it was an excellent blood vessel constrictor, reducing the amount of bleeding associated with the surgeries. With the development of many safer anesthetics, and as public awareness of cocaine's addictive qualities grew, cocaine's medical use diminished.

The most common mode of cocaine ingestion is **insufflation**, also known as **snorting**. Another mode of administration is smoking. This is not to be confused with smoking crack cocaine, which is discussed below. Until crack cocaine became available in the 1980s, snorting pure cocaine was the most common mode of usage. With the introduction of crack cocaine, smoking became a common means of introducing the drug into the system.[2]

Actual smoking of cocaine powder is not very effective in achieving the response that users desire. Unlike the amount of cocaine that actually gets into the blood following snorting, smoking it delivers only a small amount into the blood, creating a short-lived but heavy response, different from that experienced after snorting, which usually lasts 20 to 30 minutes, rising and falling once.

Cocaine powder melts at 197°C. Higher temperatures will cause the powder to evaporate, making it smokable. However, at these temperatures it burns and changes chemically so that very little actually gets absorbed through the lungs.[3] In addition, particulates released may seriously irritate the lungs. However, the throat and airways suffer more damage than the lungs do.

Some users will mix cocaine with water and inject it intravenously. The cocaine must first be treated with hydrochloric acid to make it water soluble. Then it can be mixed with the water so that the solution is not toxic (with the exception of the detrimental effects of the cocaine). This method of use is far less popular than snorting. One reason is the possible deleterious reactions that may occur when the drug is introduced directly into the blood. One of these is constriction of the blood vessels that supply the heart muscle with oxygen and nutrition.[4] This leads to changes in the blood flow to the entire body as the heart is unable to fully meet the demands of all of the tissues. It is also possible to suffer a heart attack or stroke following this method of cocaine use.

Another is the possibility of contracting diseases such as hepatitis and HIV infection from using a needle that has not been sterilized after being used by another drug user who is infected. In addition, because most intravenous drug users are not careful to use sterile techniques when injecting themselves with cocaine, the risk of abscessed infections at the injection site is greatly increased, as is damage to tissues related directly to the presence of the drug itself.

CRACK COCAINE

Approximately 100 years after cocaine began to be used by the medical profession, a modification of the compound was developed that became incredibly popular thanks to its low price tag and immediate high: crack cocaine. Also known simply as crack, this extremely addictive stimulant gets its name from the crackling sound that it makes when burned in a pipe while a user is smoking it. Crack cocaine addiction has become one of society's greatest problems.

To produce crack cocaine, simple cocaine is mixed with ammonia or sodium bicarbonate (baking soda) and water. Once heated, the mixture changes into a form that may be smoked. This process, known as "**freebasing**," makes the drug more powerful.

The use of and addiction to crack cocaine has wide-reaching effects on society. The economic costs associated with incarceration of offenders, legal representation, and time lost from work are astronomical. The increased crime rate associated with the use of the drug affects an immeasurable number of people and businesses worldwide. The number of children using crack cocaine continues to increase while the age of initial use decreases.[5]

Figure 1.3 Crack cocaine, top, is a form of cocaine that is typically smoked, as shown here at bottom. *(U.S. Drug Enforcement Administration/ © Alec Macdonald / Alamy)*

In most cases, crack is smoked using a glass handpipe or a waterpipe. Some are mass-produced in factories and others are made by users from materials that are readily available.

COMMON STREET TERMS ASSOCIATED WITH CRACK COCAINE

Street Term	Definition
badrock	crack cocaine
beautiful boulders	crack cocaine
cloud	crack cocaine
devilsmoke	crack cocaine
freebasing	smoking crack cocaine
juice joint	marijuana cigarette sprinkled with crack
lamborghini	crack pipe made from a plastic rum bottle and a rubber sparkplug cover
Mexican speedballs	crack and methamphetamine
oolies	marijuana cigarettes laced with crack
p-funk	crack mixed with PCP; heroin
perp	fake crack made of candle wax and baking soda
pimp your pipe	lending or renting crack pipe or stem
raspberry	female who trades sex for crack or money to buy crack
rock house	place where crack is sold and smoked
scrape and snort	to share crack by scraping off small pieces to snort
server	crack dealer
sheet rocking	crack and LSD
slab	a large piece of crack cocaine the size of a stick of chewing gum
space dust	crack dipped in PCP
speedboat	marijuana, PCP, and crack combined and smoked

Source: Office of National Drug Control Policy, "Street Terms: Drugs and the Drug Trade. Drug Type: Crack Cocaine," http://www.whitehousedrugpolicy.gov/streetterms/ByType.asp?intTypeID=2 (accessed March 23, 2010).

In addition to smoking crack, users will also smoke **freebase cocaine**. This is the base form of cocaine that is virtually insoluble in water, whereas **cocaine hydrochloride** is soluble. Freebasing increases the impact of the cocaine by reducing the time needed for the onset of the effects, increasing the euphoria and speeding up the "rush" experienced by the user. The same holds true for smoking crack. In both cases, the effects are shorter lived.

COCAINE AND CRACK USE AMONG YOUTH AND YOUNG ADULTS

Cocaine and crack abusers cause many difficulties for society. Use of these substances is pervasive. In 2008 a study known as "Monitoring the Future" was begun as an ongoing project to study the values, attitudes, and behaviors of American secondary school students, college students, and young adults. It is being funded by the National Institute on Drug Abuse and is conducted at the Survey Research Center in the Institute for Social Research at the University of Michigan.

Each year approximately 50,000 eighth, 10th, and 12th grade students are surveyed. In addition to the survey, in order to continue to collect reliable and relevant statistics, annual follow-up questionnaires are sent to a sample of each graduating class for several years after their initial participation.

Results from the 2009 survey showed that 1.7% of eighth graders, 2.1% of 10th graders, and 2.4% of 12th graders reported lifetime use (used at least once in the respondent's lifetime) of crack cocaine (see Table 1.1).[6] Cocaine is used by eighth, 10th, and 12th graders with more frequency than crack cocaine, with 6% of 12th graders reporting having used cocaine at least once in their lifetime (see Table 1.2).

Table 1.1 Crack Cocaine Use by Students, 2009 Monitoring the Future Survey			
	8th Graders	10th Graders	12th Graders
Lifetime	1.7%	2.1%	2.4%
Past Year	1.1	1.2	1.3
Past Month	0.5	0.4	0.6
Source: National Institute on Drug Abuse, "NIDA InfoFacts: Cocaine," http://www.drugabuse. gov/Infofacts/cocaine.html (accessed May 18, 2010).			

Table 1.2 Cocaine Use by Students, 2008 Monitoring the Future Survey

	8th Graders	10th Graders	12th Graders
Lifetime	2.6%	4.6%	6.0%
Past Year	1.6	2.7	3.4
Past Month	0.8	0.9	1.3

Source: National Institute on Drug Abuse, "NIDA InfoFacts: Cocaine," http://www.drugabuse. gov/Infofacts/cocaine.html (accessed May 18, 2010).

Table 1.3 Percent of Students Reporting Risk of Using Crack Cocaine, 2008

Say "great risk" to:	8th Grade	10th Grade	12th Grade
Try crack once/twice	47.1%	56.5%	47.5%
Take crack occasionally	67.9	76.5	65.2
Try powder cocaine once/twice	42.7	49.8	45.1
Take powder cocaine occasionally	62.7	71.1	61.6

Sources: Office of National Drug Control Policy, "Crack Facts and Figures," http://www. whitehousedrugpolicy.gov/drugfact/crack/crack_ff.html (accessed May 18, 2010);Office of National Drug Control Policy, "Cocaine Facts and Figures," http://www.whitehousedrugpolicy. gov/drugfact/cocaine/cocaine_ff.html (accessed on May 25, 2010).

Table 1.4 Percent of College Students/Young Adults Reporting Cocaine/Crack Use, 2007

	College Students		Young Adults	
	Cocaine	Crack	Cocaine	Crack
Past month	1.7%	0.1%	2.1%	0.3%
Past year	5.4	0.6	6.2	1.0
Lifetime	8.5	1.3	14.7	3.9

Source: National Institute on Drug Abuse, "Monitoring the Future National Survey Results on Drug Use, 1975–2007. Volume II: College Students & Adults Ages 19–45," http://www. monitoringthefuture.org/pubs/monographs/vol2_2007.pdf (accessed May 18, 2010).

It is interesting to note that approximately 67.9% of eighth graders, 76.5% of 10th graders, and 65.2% of 12th graders surveyed in 2008 reported that taking crack cocaine occasionally was a "great risk." When surveyed, these same students were also asked if using crack cocaine only once or twice was also a "great risk." When questioned on whether or not using cocaine posed a "great risk," these students answered similarly.[7] The results of this survey are seen in Table 1.3.

Possibly the most unnerving statistics associated with this study are those obtained by the survey as it related to college students and young adults aged 19–28. College students actually showed a lower percentage of lifetime use of crack cocaine than did the eighth, 10th, or 12th graders. However, use of crack cocaine by young adults was two to three times greater than that of college students. Approximately 1.3% of college students and 3.9% of young adults (ages 19–28) surveyed in 2007 reported lifetime use of crack cocaine. Table 1.4 shows these results.

History of Cocaine and Crack

Mark was looking forward to his excursion to the Andes Mountains in Peru during his summer break from teaching archaeology at the university. He hoped to find some interesting artifacts while exploring the outskirts of several villages located at high altitudes.

Once he arrived in Huaráz, he was excited to begin his trek. However, he noticed that he was feeling rather tired as well as suffering a headache. In addition, he was somewhat light-headed and had some mild feelings of pins and needles in his hands and feet.

Mark's guide, Eduardo, knew just what was happening. Mark was suffering from altitude sickness. This is a common problem for people who have come from lower altitudes where the air pressure is greater than it is in Huaráz, which is located at an altitude of over 10,000 feet above sea level.

Eduardo had the answer for Mark's problem. He reached into his pocket and pulled out his chuspa. This is a woven pouch that holds coca leaves mixed with llipta, ashes from a quinoa plant. The llipta is mixed with the coca leaves to soften their effects. The concoction is used to overcome the effects of altitude sickness and has been used for centuries in roughly the same form. Eduardo instructed Mark to sit down and chew.

Mark soon began to experience a mild tingling sensation in his mouth. However, his headache subsided, he began to feel more energized, the pins and needles disappeared, and he became less short of breath. He did not become "high" because the amount of cocaine in coca

leaves is only around 0.8 percent, which will not cause the typical effects
experienced with pure cocaine use. Now he was ready to start his trek
through the mountains in search of artifacts he might bring back to his
classes at the university.

HISTORIC USE OF COCAINE

Cocaine has been used for centuries in its natural form, coca leaves. The plant,
Erythroxylum coca, grows in South America and has been a significant part of
traditional Andean culture since at least the sixth century.[1] Originally it was
used by Incan nobles and a few select groups such as couriers, members of the
military, court orators, and favored public workers. In later years the practice
of chewing the leaves spread to the public after the Incan empire declined and
the Spanish began inhabiting the area.

Coca was introduced to Europe by soldiers returning from the New
World in the sixteenth century, but became popular in the mid-nineteenth
century when Dr. Paolo Montegazza wrote a paper that touted coca's ability to
increase cognition. In order to make using the leaves easier, Angelo Mariani,
a chemist, created **Vin Mariani** in 1863. This was a Bordeaux wine treated
with coca leaves. Mariani was greatly influenced by Montegazza's paper. The
alcohol in the wine extracted the cocaine from the leaves so that the wine
contained 6 milligrams of cocaine per ounce. The wine was so popular that
Pope Leo XIII drank it, and he awarded the wine a Vatican Gold Medal and
appeared on a poster to endorse the wine.[2] In addition, many world leaders
also drank the wine.

In addition to wines fortified with coca leaves, coca was added to other
products, most of them sold as elixirs and patent medicines. One of the most
famous products that included coca was the original version of Coca-Cola.
It appeared in 1886 as another form of coca wine similar to Vin Mariani and
was touted as a cure for a number of diseases, including morphine addiction and impotence. Eventually it became a carbonated beverage sold at soda
fountains because it was believed that carbonated water was good for one's
health. In 1906 the passage of the Pure Food and Drug Act made illegal the
use of coca in foods, and the Coca-Cola formula had to be changed.

Cocaine's chemical name is benzoylmethylecgonine. Its actual name is a
combination of the word *coca,* the source of the chemical, and the suffix "-ine,"
which is used to identify an alkaloid, the chemical family to which cocaine

belongs. Alkaloids are chemical compounds that contain basic nitrogen atoms. Cocaine is in the **tropane** group of alkaloids, which includes atropine, scopolamine, and others.

Figure 2.1   Vin Mariani.   *(National Library of Medicine)*

Although the stimulatory effects of cocaine were well known for centuries by cultures that used the coca plant, isolation of the actual chemical did not occur until 1855 when the German chemist Friedrich Gaedcke isolated the cocaine alkaloid thanks to advances in the knowledge of chemistry. He named the compound **erythroxyline** (from the genus name for coca). One of the reasons that it took so many years to identify the active ingredient of coca plants was that the research was being done in Europe and not in South America where the plant was grown. In the time it took for the plants to be transported from South America to Europe, many of them were damaged and there was much chemical breakdown.

In 1859 Albert Niemann, a Ph.D. student at the University of Göttingen, in Germany, received a trunk full of coca leaves that had been transported aboard the *Novara,* an Austrian frigate that was commissioned by Emperor Franz Josef to circle the world. He was able to develop an improved purification process for cocaine.[3] Cocaine was finally synthesized from **tropinone**, a chemically related natural compound, in 1898 by Richard Willstätter.[4]

In the mid to late 1800s, cocaine was used for a variety of medical treatments, including morphine addiction, overcoming exhaustion, local anesthesia (particularly in the mouth and eyes), and numerous other conditions. In 1884 Sigmund Freud wrote his first scientific paper, "Über Coca" ("About Cocaine"), praising cocaine and listing the many ailments that he believed cocaine could successfully treat.[5] These afflictions included fatigue, asthma, indigestion, emaciation, morphine addiction, alcoholism, depression, autism, and lack of sexual appetite. When challenged by other psychiatrists, Freud quickly leaped to cocaine's defense.

By 1885 the Parke-Davis pharmaceutical company made cocaine available to the public in a number of different forms. It offered for sale cigarettes, powder, and a liquid form that was to be injected directly into a vein. The package even included the needle.

Cocaine use was written about in many books, articles, journals, and songs. Sir Arthur Conan Doyle included its use in his stories of the renowned detective Sherlock Holmes, who often resorted to injecting cocaine when he was bored. Songwriter Cole Porter, in his song "I Get a Kick Out of You," included the line, "Some get a kick from cocaine." Rock guitarist Eric Clapton performed Grammy Award–winning songwriter J. J. Cale's hit song "Cocaine."

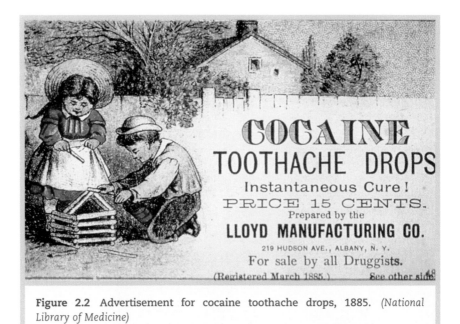

Figure 2.2 Advertisement for cocaine toothache drops, 1885. *(National Library of Medicine)*

As available to the public as simple aspirin was, cocaine was sold in drugstores in the early twentieth century for five to ten cents for a small boxful. White employers encouraged their black laborers to use it so that their productivity would increase, and stevedores along the Mississippi River used the drug for the same reason.[6]

By the beginning of the twentieth century, the addictive properties of cocaine were evident and public and governmental concern was on the rise. In an article in the *American Journal of Pharmacy* in 1903, it was stated that most users of cocaine were "Bohemians, gamblers, high-and low-class prostitutes, night porters, bell boys, burglars, racketeers, pimps, and casual laborers."[7] This was not entirely accurate, but it still helped to support the growing fear that cocaine use would lead to serious problems in society.

On December 17, 1914, the U.S. Congress passed the Harrison Narcotics Tax Act, which taxed and regulated the production, importation, and distribution of opiates. A passage that referred directly to cocaine read, "An Act To provide for the registration of, with collectors of internal revenue, and to

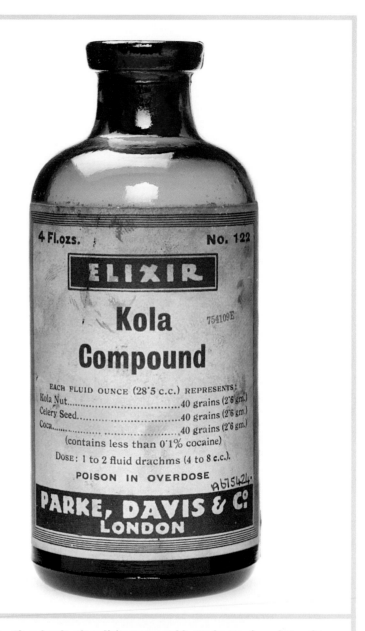

Figure 2.3   Glass bottle of medicine prepared by Parke, Davis and Co. of London. The ingredients include kola nut, celery seed, and coca (from which cocaine is derived).   *(© Getty Images)*

impose a special tax on all persons who produce, import, manufacture, compound, deal in, dispense, sell, distribute, or give away opium or coca leaves, their salts, derivatives, or preparations, and for other purposes."[8] The act required doctors, pharmacists, and others who prescribed narcotics to register and pay a tax.[9] The public could no longer obtain cocaine legally without a doctor's help. Cocaine finally became a controlled substance in the United States in 1970 when Congress passed the Controlled Substances Act.

Currently, cocaine is used illegally by many individuals throughout the world. It is particularly popular among individuals with high incomes due to its expense. However, its use is not limited to this socioeconomic group, and it is often linked to crimes committed to support a poorer individual's habit.

Dealers will often "cut" or "step on" pure cocaine with inactive, inexpensive substances to increase profits. These include sugars such as powdered sugar, mannitol, and glucose; creatine (an organic acid used to supply energy to muscles); bicarbonate of soda; starch; powdered vitamins; Epsom salts; quinine; or any other cheap, harmless substance. In addition, cocaine is also cut with procaine and benzocaine, local anesthetics that increase its numbing property, powdered methamphetamine, ephedrine, and caffeine to increase its stimulatory effects, and **levamisole**, a drug used to treat worms in humans and animals that also apparently enhances the psychoactive effects of cocaine. In fact, federal agents found that 69 percent of cocaine shipments seized entering the United States were cut with levamisole.[10] A study by the European Monitoring Centre for Drugs and Drug Addiction in 2007 revealed that, on average, cocaine bought on the streets is less than 50% pure.[11]

HISTORIC USE OF CRACK

Crack's history is not as old as that of the cocaine from which it is created. It made its first appearance mainly in the poor neighborhoods of Miami, Los Angeles, and New York in 1984.[12] Crack cocaine is a freebase form of cocaine. That is, it is the pure basic from of cocaine rather than its salt. It derives its name from the crackling sound heard while it is being smoked in a crack pipe.

Crack's appearance and increased use in the 1980s came about mainly because it was easy to make, the high provided by smoking it came on very quickly and was more intense than that provided by cocaine, and it was considerably cheaper than cocaine. Between 1986 and 1992 news coverage about crack was widespread as there was increasing fear of a crack "epidemic" in the ghettos.[13]

It became clear to the U.S. government that cocaine was not simply a recreational drug used by the rich and famous. Indeed, it was a damaging substance that caused bodily harm and led to serious increases in crime, particularly when it was turned into crack. Thus, Congress passed the Anti-Drug Abuse Acts of 1986 and 1988, establishing severe punishments for individuals using or selling either substance.

The 1986 act gave the government more power to stop the importation and trafficking of cocaine to be used for crack production. Increased tariffs were placed on goods imported from countries that did not cooperate in controlling the export of cocaine, seizure of property of drug offenders became easier, and mandatory prison sentences for possession were reinstated.

It soon became evident that most of the offenders sentenced under the provisions relating to crack were African American, while sentences related to powder cocaine use were mainly handed down to white lawbreakers. However, mandatory minimum sentencing associated with the amount of the specific drug possessed was different for crack than it was for cocaine, and most crack use was among African Americans in the ghettos. Basically, there was a 100 to 1 sentencing disparity between the two. The same jail term, a 10-year minimum sentence, would be applied to possession of 50 grams of crack or 5,000 grams of powder cocaine. Some believed the disparity was a function of race discrimination, but the government justified this difference by saying that crack use was more widespread, it provided a more intense effect than cocaine, and it sold more cheaply.

The Anti-Drug Abuse Act of 1988 went further in its attempt to deter the possession, use, and trafficking of cocaine and crack, as well as other illegal drugs, by assigning the death penalty to those who were linked to a death associated with these drugs.[14]

The specific inventor of crack cocaine is not known. The factors that contribute to the preferred use of crack over powdered cocaine are clear. Powdered cocaine is difficult to handle whereas crack comes in a hard, rock-like form that is easily transported, smoked, and concealed. Powdered cocaine is either inhaled nasally, smoked, or injected. This can lead to serious damage to the nasal passages, lung damage, or a number of very dangerous rections brought about by the use of hypodermic needles. It is also much more expensive than crack, thus limiting its appeal to the average user. In addition, because cocaine is cut with any number of substances to raise profits, the user may be exposed to chemicals that will cause serious bodily harm or even death. Lastly, free-basing cocaine is a dangerous process that often uses ether, which is highly flammable. Explosions during the process are not uncommon. Using crack overcomes these problems, which makes it more popular. It is easily made into the rock-like form by a simple process using household items.

Perhaps two of the most infamous figures associated with cocaine and crack are Ricky Donnell Ross and Oscar Danilo Blandón. Ross has been cred-ited with being the source of the crack epidemic in South Central Los Angeles in the early 1980s. He was able to buy much of his cocaine from Blandón, the former head of Nicaragua's agricultural imports, who was linked to the con-tras, an anticommunist "army" in Nicaragua that allegedly received much of its funding from the sale of cocaine and crack in the United States during that time period. After many investigations, Ross was incarcerated in prison and received parole on September 29, 2009. Blandón helped to get Ross convicted and was sentenced to 24 months in prison for his involvement in bringing cocaine to Los Angeles. His sentence was modified to time already served and a $50 fine[17] and he was given a job with the U.S. Drug Enforcement Agency (DEA).[15] He was the only known foreigner ever convicted of drug trafficking who was not deported.

3
How Cocaine and Crack Work

The party was getting underway and Liz was feeling somewhat apprehensive. It was the first time that she would snort cocaine and she wondered how her body would react to a substance that, based on what she had read and observed, she knew would have a powerful effect on her mood. Nevertheless, she had always been intrigued by the notion of experiencing the great high she was certain she would feel.

Her friend Kimberly reassured her that it would be one of the greatest experiences of her life, so she set up a line of cocaine on a pocket mirror and handed Liz a short plastic drinking straw. Liz was a bit shaky as she placed the straw in her nose and began to inhale through it and move it along the line of white powder.

In a very short time, Liz began to feel an intense euphoria accompanied by a heightening of her senses. She was very happy with her life and wanted to talk about it with everyone around her. She was sure that she had made the right decision to use the cocaine and was filled with an energy she had never before experienced. All of those around her who were also snorting were experiencing the same feelings to varying degrees. This was a night that would change Liz's life.

Cocaine has a direct effect on the nervous system. After a person snorts cocaine or smokes crack, cocaine molecules get into the bloodstream and quickly (within seconds) enter the brain by crossing the **blood-brain barrier**. This is a protective mechanism that has developed within the brain to keep out harmful substances that are circulating in the bloodstream. It is made up of tight junctions (cells packed closely together) of **endothelial cells**, which line the capillaries that feed the brain. Only small molecules (fat-soluble or **hydrophobic**, as in hormones) or those with a transport protein (such as glucose) are able to cross the barrier and enter the brain tissue. Because cocaine use leads to an increase in the available amount of the **neurotransmitters dopamine, serotonin, norepinephrine**, and **glutamate**, the pleasurable sensations, changes in behavior, and development of addiction all evolve with continued use. Addiction does not necessarily develop after an individual's first exposure to cocaine and crack, but thanks to the powerful feelings of euphoria and stimulation, it is not surprising that a large number of first-time users go on to continue their use, often to the point of addiction.

Immediate physiological responses to use of cocaine and crack include an increase in body temperature, heart rate, and blood pressure. Blood vessels become constricted and the pupils dilate. It is not uncommon for the user to experience headaches as well as abdominal pains and nausea. Cocaine and crack's ability to reduce the appetite often leads to the individual becoming malnourished. The degree to which each individual user experiences these effects will vary based on many factors. For example, cocaine and crack users who are experienced will need larger doses to achieve the same levels of a high that they had previously sustained. The purity of the cocaine or crack will also have a bearing on the sensations the individual experiences. The larger the content or the purer the cocaine snorted or used to make the crack, the more intense the high will be. Additionally, the route of administration will also affect how an individual reacts to cocaine.

STRUCTURE AND FUNCTION OF THE NERVOUS SYSTEM

The nervous system is divided into two anatomical components: The central nervous system (CNS), which consists of the brain and spinal cord, and the **peripheral nervous system (PNS)**, which includes all other nerves in the body. The CNS is where cocaine and crack have their effects.

The human brain contains approximately 100 billion neurons (nerves) and about 150 trillion synapses (the contact points between nerves, discussed later in this chapter).[1] The **cortex**, the region of the brain that makes up most of its mass, is divided into two hemispheres, left and right. This is the area of the brain that is responsible for thinking, reasoning, interpretation of senses, artistic appreciation, and a host of other functions.

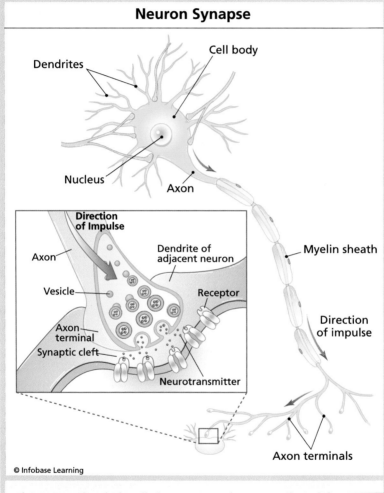

Neuron Synapse

© Infobase Learning

Figure 3.1 Chemicals called neurotransmitters are released from one neuron and travel across the neuron synapse to a receiving neuron, thereby passing messages in the brain. Cocaine causes an excess release of neurotransmitters like dopamine into the synapse and blocks reuptake of the dopamine, resulting in a flooding of synapses in the brain with dopamine.

The two hemispheres are connected by the **corpus callosum**, a structure made of nerve fibers covered with a fatty substance called **myelin** that helps nerves conduct impulses faster. All of the brain's activity is carried out by the billions of neurons that it contains. Each neuron communicates with other neurons at a junction known as the **synapse**. Here, chemicals called neurotransmitters fill the synapse gap so that nerve impulses may cross the space from one nerve to another or from a nerve to a muscle. In this way, the impulse can travel to its endpoint to cause a response in a muscle, gland, or organ, or carry out communication in the brain.

Because the brain has so many synapses and several of these neurotransmitters, many drugs may be used therapeutically in different areas to bring about changes in the behavior of an individual. These drugs target the neurotransmitters themselves or they may mimic them so that a modification of the nerve impulse takes place. This activity is what hopefully brings about the desired change in behavior. Cocaine and crack, even though they are not prescribed to treat a specific condition, will also alter a person's behavior in much the same way as legitimately prescribed psychotropic drugs.

The mechanism whereby a nerve impulse is generated from one nerve to the next is very functional. A nerve impulse is carried along the axon of the **presynaptic neuron** (the nerve before the synapse) due to chemical changes that relate particularly to the minerals sodium and potassium. At the end of the axon are axon terminals that contain vesicles filled with a specific neurotransmitter. Just beyond these terminals is a space, the synapse, which must be filled with

Table 3.1 How Different Routes of Administration Determine the Timing of the Effects of Cocaine and Crack				
Route	Onset	Peak Effect (min)	Duration (min)	Half-Life (min)
Inhalation	7 seconds	1–5	20	40–60
Intravenous	15 seconds	3–5	20–30	40–60
Nasal	3 minutes	15	45–90	60–90
Oral	10 minutes	60	60	60–90

Source: Lynn Barkley Burnett, Carlos J. Roldan, and Jonathan Adler, "Toxicity, Cocaine," eMedicine, March 19, 2010, http://emedicine.medscape.com/article/813959-overview.

neurotransmitters so that the impulse can jump across and continue through the next nerve, the **postsynaptic neuron** (the nerve after the synapse).

The dendrites (small projections radiating from the nerve cell body) of this postsynaptic neuron contain receptors designed to capture the specific neurotransmitter, thus allowing the impulse to continue on its journey. Once the impulse stops, the neurotransmitter must be removed from the synapse. This takes place in one of three ways, depending on the location of the synapse. For example, at the neuromuscular junction, the region where a nerve meets a muscle's motor endplate to stimulate contraction of the muscle, an enzyme known as **acetylcholinesterase** will digest the neurotransmitter **acetylcholine**. In other synapses, simple diffusion (movement of the neurotransmitter molecules from a higher to a lower concentration) takes place.

In the brain, removal of the neurotransmitters is achieved by **reuptake transporters** that carry the neurotransmitter back into the axon terminal. This is where cocaine does its work. It interferes with the reuptake transporters for dopamine, serotonin, and norepinephrine, which are then allowed to remain in the synapse, leading to continued transmission of impulses. This will modify a person's behavior because behavior is based on the numerous impulses that are transmitted from nerve to nerve through the synapses. There are several neurotransmitters in the brain and all of them may be affected by a variety of drugs.

This scenario of nerve impulse transmission takes place constantly throughout the body as long as an individual is alive. It is the center of the mechanism used to run the body's muscles, organs, and glands, and the functions of the brain and spinal cord. The nervous system works closely with the endocrine system, which is responsible for the secretion of many hormones. Together, they are often referred to as the **neuroendocrine system**.

HOW COCAINE AND CRACK AFFECT THE NERVOUS SYSTEM

Cocaine and crack affect the nervous system by interfering with the neurotransmitter reuptake process in the brain. Some drugs will act by disrupting only one of the neurotransmitters in the brain. Cocaine and crack inhibit dopamine reuptake, causing the feelings of euphoria associated with their use.

Table 3.2 Neurotransmitters, Their Locations, What They Do, and Drugs That Affect Their Actions			
Neurotransmitter	Distribution in the Central Nervous System	Functions Affected	Drugs That Affect
Dopamine	Midbrain Ventral tegmental area (VTA) Cerebral cortex Hypothalamus	Pleasure and reward Movement Attention Memory	Cocaine Metham- phetamine Amphetamine (Most drugs of abuse directly or indirectly aug- ment dopamine in the reward pathway)
Glutamate	Widely distributed in brain	Neuron activity (increased rate) Learning Cognition Memory	Cocaine Ketamine Phencyclidine Alcohol
Norepinephrine	Midbrain VTA Cerebral cortex Hypothalamus	Sensory processing Movement Sleep Mood Memory Anxiety	Cocaine Methamphet- amine Amphetamine
Serotonin	Midbrain VTA Cerebral cortex Hypothalamus	Mood Sleep Sexual desire Appetite	MDMA (ecstasy) LSD Cocaine

Source: Carl Sherman, "Impacts of Drugs on Neurotransmission," NIDA Notes, October 2007, http://www.drugabuse.gov/NIDA_notes/NNvol21N4/Impacts.html (accessed January 18, 2011).

They also inhibit reuptake of norepinephrine and serotonin and bring about release of glutamate, leading to the stimulation associated with their use.

Cocaine binds strongly to the synaptic reuptake transporters for dopamine, norepinephrine, and serotonin. This causes them to remain in their respective synapses and allows nerve transmission to continue after it would have normally stopped. In addition, it also causes an increased release of the three neurotransmitters into the synapses. Thus, cocaine and crack provide a two-pronged approach leading to a significant increase in neurotransmitters that brings about a powerful euphoria and considerable stimulation.

Cocaine's mode of action on glutamate activity is somewhat different, but still involves its effect on dopamine. Glutamate is the most abundant excitatory neurotransmitter in the brain.[2] It is involved in learning and memory. Addiction is a form of learning wherein the individual makes the association of the enjoyable experiences of euphoria and stimulation with the use of crack or cocaine.

In the **ventral tegmental area** (VTA) of the brain, an area associated with the reward system, cocaine affects dopamine neurons, making them more sensitive to glutamate. This is in addition to its blocking of reuptake transporters for the dopamine. The neurons become hypersensitive to the

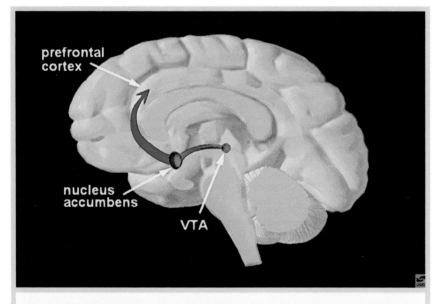

Figure 3.2 The reward system in the brain originates in a group of neurons in the midbrain called the ventral tegmental area (VTA). When cocaine molecules bind to the neurons of the VTA, the neurons release dopamine into the prefrontal cortex and nucleus accumbens. It is this release of dopamine into the nucleus accumbens that produces the overall feeling of pleasure in the cocaine or crack user. *(National Institute on Drug Abuse)*

STEP-BY-STEP MODE OF ACTION OF COCAINE AND CRACK

1) Cocaine is snorted or smoked and is absorbed into the bloodstream or is injected directly.
2) The drug travels to the brain where it affects the dopamine-rich areas (nucleus accumbens, VTA, and caudate nucleus—all parts of the "reward pathway") by blocking dopamine reuptake transporters.
3) The blocking allows dopamine to remain in the synapse for an extended length of time, thus allowing continued nerve impulse transmission.
4) These continued impulses in this region of the brain cause the user to experience euphoria and the "high" associated with cocaine and crack usage.

Source: The Lundbeck Institute, "The Mechanism of Action of Cocaine," http://www.cnsforum.com/imagebank/item/MAO_cocaine/default.aspx (accessed October 19, 2010).

cocaine, resulting in addiction. The person continues to seek out the drug in an effort to reproduce the extremely positive results he or she experienced. Unfortunately, this search becomes extremely obsessive and compulsive.

Cocaine also has an effect in the **nucleus accumbens** and the **prefrontal cortex**. The nucleus accumbens is a pleasure and reward center in the brain that is directly connected to the VTA by nerves that secrete the neurotransmitter dopamine. Dopamine excites the action of the nucleus accumbens, so when cocaine is used and blocks reuptake of dopamine, the extra neurotransmitter available excites this region to a greater degree. In addition, cocaine also inhibits the reuptake of serotonin. This neurotransmitter also has an excitatory effect on the nucleus accumbens, which means that the excess serotonin will stimulate this area of the brain, bringing about the pleasurable sensations that lead to addiction.[3] Thus, the combination of additional dopamine and serotonin will cause the individual to experience an exceptionally strong feeling of euphoria and well-being.

The prefrontal cortex is responsible for decision making and moderating correct social behavior. It has a direct connection to the **limbic system**, which is an important seat of emotions. Thanks to inhibition of the limbic system by the prefrontal cortex, normal individuals will control their anger and other strong emotions under most circumstances. However, when the neurons of the prefrontal cortex are exposed to cocaine, glutamate transmission in the nucleus accumbens is increased. Since this neurotransmitter is excitatory, there is an increase in cocaine-seeking behavior and a continuation of the addiction process.[4]

USING COCAINE AND CRACK WITH OTHER DRUGS

An interesting interrelationship between cocaine and nicotine has been noted. Nicotine is known to increase dopamine levels in the brain. Since cocaine also acts to increase available dopamine in the synapses, many cocaine users who also smoke at the same time as using cocaine have reported an increase in the feelings of euphoria experienced while snorting cocaine or smoking crack.[5] One of the common problems faced by users who engage in both practices at the same time is an uncontrollable urge to chain smoke. This creates a problem for the cardiovascular system as the stimulatory effects of the cocaine coupled with those of nicotine can put a great strain on the heart.

Smoking crack or snorting or injecting cocaine simultaneously with alcohol presents a similar problem. When cocaine is taken with alcohol, the two will combine in the liver to form **cocaethylene** (ethylbenzoylecgonine). This substance creates a greater level of euphoria than cocaine alone and it is also more toxic to the cardiovascular system. In addition, drinking alcohol prior to using cocaine or crack increases the bioavailability of cocaine. So, once again, users will tend to combine alcohol with cocaine and crack in an effort to achieve a greater high, while putting themselves at a more significant risk. It has been suggested that the combined use of alcohol and cocaine may be the most common cause of drug-related deaths.[6] In addition, most concurrent use of illicit or prescribed drugs occurs with alcohol. The most widespread occurrence of this is among 12- to 17-year-olds. The incidence declines as individuals get older.

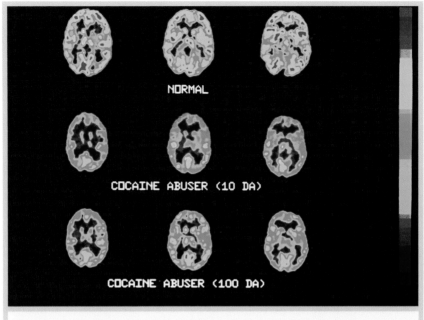

NORMAL

COCAINE ABUSER (10 DA)

COCAINE ABUSER (100 DA)

Figure 3.3   A normal brain (top) and a cocaine abuser's brain 10 and 100 days after taking the drug. Normal metabolic activity, indicated by bright red and yellow, is blunted in the drug abuser. *(© Brookhaven National Laboratory/ Photo Researchers, Inc.)*

Some users will combine cocaine with heroin in a combination known as a "**speedball**." Speedballing involves the snorting or injecting of heroin immediately followed by smoking of cocaine or crack. This causes an enhancement of the effects of both drugs. In addition, individuals addicted to crack may use heroin to reduce the effects of crack **withdrawal** or the agitation produced by extended crack use.

Several different chemicals and drugs, in addition to alcohol and nicotine, have the ability to heighten the effects of cocaine and crack. **Organophosphates**, originally developed to be used as nerve gases, are now widely used as insecticides and fire retardants. They have very powerful neurotoxic effects and must be used with caution. Cocaine and crack users who use these chemicals do so because they inhibit the enzyme **pseudocholinesterase**, which helps the body break down cocaine. Inhibiting the enzyme makes the effects of cocaine and crack last longer, extending the time that the person may experience their effects.

Phenytoin is a prescription antiepileptic drug that is also used to treat some cardiac arrhythmias (irregular heartbeats) and a condition known as trigeminal neuralgia, which is severe nerve pain associated with one of the cranial nerves. It acts by inhibiting electrical conductance between brain cells. When taken with cocaine or crack, the intoxication experience is enhanced.

Dangerous effects result from the concurrent use of cocaine and crack with antidepressants such as **monoamine oxidase inhibitors** (MAOIs) and **tricyclic antidepressants** (TCAs), the antihypertensive drug **alpha-methyldopa**, and **reserpine**, which is both an antihypertensive and antipsychotic drug. Each of these medications interferes with the reuptake of serotonin, dopamine, and norepinephrine, so the effects of cocaine and crack are greatly enhanced. This leads to an **adrenergic crisis** wherein the individual suffers with a very rapid heart rate (**tachycardia**) and severely elevated blood pressure. If a person already has an underlying heart condition or hypertension, the effects could easily be fatal.

It is important to understand that, in many cases, the cocaine or crack user is unaware that he or she is taking an impure product as many dealers "cut" the cocaine and crack with other substances in order to increase profits. Some of the chemicals used for this are local anesthetics such as lidocaine, procaine, and tetracaine, stimulants such as amphetamine, caffeine, and methylphenidate, and other substances such as lysergic acid diethylamide (LSD), phencyclidine (PCP), phenytoin, heroin, marijuana, hashish, and the veterinary dewormer levamisole, which also increases dopamine levels.[7]

4
Addiction to Cocaine and Crack

Bernie, who was only 19 years old, had been smoking crack for four years. He was introduced to it by one of the older kids in the neighborhood who convinced him that he would never experience a greater feeling than that which he was about to feel. He went along with it and found that, from that point on, he was unable to avoid smoking crack and that he developed a powerful craving for it.

Bernie began to notice that he felt the need to smoke frequently as he would suffer from serious depression if he went too long without getting his "fix." He considered himself lucky that it didn't cost too much to buy some rocks and smoke several times each day. He often wondered how he would continue to feel good if he lost the menial job he had that supplied him with sufficient funds to maintain his habit.

As long as he was smoking, he felt as if he could conquer the world. He had great plans for what he was going to do with his life, places he would visit all over the world and how he would most likely one day become the CEO of a major corporation so he would never have to worry about money again.

If too much time elapsed between "hits," he would become irritable and get angry following the slightest provocation. He was also extremely tired and found himself sleeping a lot unless he was smoking. His appetite also diminished and he lost quite a bit of weight during the four years that he was smoking crack regularly. He also didn't bother to shower often nor worry about how his hair or clothing looked.

What happened to Bernie during the four years that he was addicted to crack cocaine is typical of what happens to most crack and cocaine addicts. Because cocaine in any form causes the neurotransmitter dopamine to remain in the synapses of the brain for an extended length of time, users experience euphoria, a very pleasurable experience. In addition, they also become extremely confident in themselves and experience delusions of grandeur.

Unfortunately, as users continue to abuse cocaine and crack, the highs that they experience become increasingly difficult to achieve at the levels of the drug they started at in the first place. This event is called **tachyphylaxis**. It tends to develop in virtually all drug addicts and also among individuals that are taking any number of prescription medications not related to psychotropic drugs for numerous conditions. Over time, the body becomes desensitized to the drug being taken. This is often caused by a considerable reduction or depletion in the amount of neurotransmitter available in the synapse that is bringing about the desired effect. This desensitization often develops due to a high-intensity prolonged stimulus or a lower-level repeated stimulus from the drug being used or abused.

HOW USE LEADS TO ADDICTION

Once an individual begins to use cocaine or crack, he or she is at great risk of becoming an addict. Both forms of cocaine are associated with a high degree of rapid addiction. Objectively, it is easy to see why a person can become addicted when the effects of a "hit" are analyzed.

Immediately following the snorting of cocaine, the user will experience very powerful effects that last for about ten minutes. The intensity of these effects will vary depending on the quality and quantity of the cocaine and on the individual's reactions to the substance. The effects peak immediately, but don't last for a long time.

In the first 15 minutes, cocaine causes a sensation of euphoria and well-being. This is accompanied by very strong physical, mental, and sensory stimulation. The user feels more alert than usual and is more precise in movements. In addition, there may be a distortion of hearing, touch, and sight.

It is not unusual to experience a mild numbness of the gums and nasal cavities when cocaine is snorted. Eventually, this extends to the sinuses. Right after this occurs, the user enters a phase of euphoria in which his or her personality is intensified and there is an overestimation of reactions accompanied by hypercommunicability. Users feel that they understand everything, and it is not uncommon to become less sensitive to pain, fatigue, and hunger. Finally, there is a strong sense of lack of appetite because cocaine is an appetite suppressant.

The effects of using cocaine usually last for one or two hours followed by a comedown that is instantaneous. This is associated with a change of the euphoria into sleepiness, mild depression, and slower reflexes. With regular use, the symptoms of this phase continue to become stronger.[1]

The initial experience brings with it an intense sense of pleasure. It is the kind of sensation that the brain would surely wish to repeat. Unfortunately, because of the areas of the brain that are stimulated by the use of crack and cocaine, addiction is the usual result.

MECHANISM OF ADDICTION

Once cocaine crosses the blood-brain barrier and enters the brain, it causes an increase in the amount of the neurotransmitter dopamine in the synapses thanks to its ability to block reuptake transporters. Because dopamine is directly responsible for activating the pleasure and reward circuits of the brain, the user experiences an extremely uplifting feeling of euphoria. These centers are designed to activate during certain pleasurable activities such as eating and sex. It is because of this activation that people are driven to repeat the action that brought about the pleasurable feelings.

The concept of **drug addiction** is defined in many different ways. Psychiatric professionals define it as "a pattern of substance use leading to significant impairment in function."[2] It is often equated to **substance dependence**. In order for a health care professional to make a diagnosis of substance dependence, the patient being examined must demonstrate the persistent use of alcohol or other drugs despite experiencing problems related to the use of the substance or substances in question. Compulsive and repetitive use of the drug or drugs may lead to tolerance of the

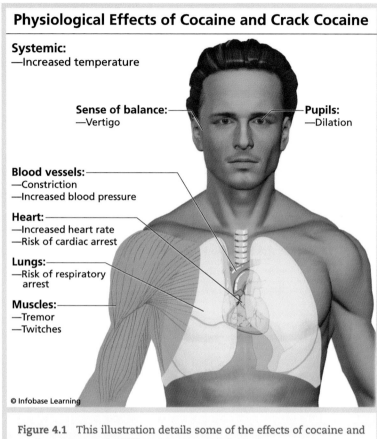

Physiological Effects of Cocaine and Crack Cocaine

Systemic:
—Increased temperature

Sense of balance:
—Vertigo

Pupils:
—Dilation

Blood vessels:
—Constriction
—Increased blood pressure

Heart:
—Increased heart rate
—Risk of cardiac arrest

Lungs:
—Risk of respiratory
  arrest

Muscles:
—Tremor
—Twitches

© Infobase Learning

Figure 4.1   This illustration details some of the effects of cocaine and crack cocaine on the different systems of the body.

effects of the substance as well as serious withdrawal symptoms when use is reduced or stopped. This and substance abuse are considered substance use disorders.[3]

One of the components of addiction is **physical dependence**. This develops due to chronic use of a drug, in this case cocaine or crack, causing tolerance, or tachyphylaxis, as described above. Individuals who are dependent will suffer from withdrawal symptoms when the cocaine or crack are abruptly withdrawn.

With continued use of cocaine or crack, and the prolonged time period that dopamine remains in the synapses, the brain adapts to these elevated levels and the amount of dopamine produced decreases. Between uses of cocaine or crack, the user experiences fatigue, depression, and altered moods. This acts to drive the individual to seek out cocaine or crack to counteract these symptoms.

Drug addiction occurs in three stages, according to the American Psychiatric Association's *Diagnostic and Statistical Manual of Mental Disorders, Fourth Edition—Text Revision* (*DSM-IV-TR*) : preoccupation/anticipation, binge/intoxication, and withdrawal.[4]

In the preoccupation/anticipation stage, the user has a constant **craving** for the cocaine or crack. No matter what responsibilities or activities he or she is engaged in, there is a constant preoccupation to obtain and use the drug. An almost constant state of fatigue, depression, irritability, agitation, and difficulty concentrating plague the user. The individual is always distracted by his or her preoccupation with obtaining the crack or cocaine. He or she often finds it difficult to properly perform various tasks that require concentration and a clear head.

In the binge/intoxication stage, the user finds it necessary to use increasingly larger doses of cocaine or crack in order to achieve the high that was initially attained. This leads to excessive use of the substances, or bingeing. At this point the effects of the intoxication become extremely dangerous. As the user continues in this direction, desensitization occurs. This often leads to overdosing as the user attempts to achieve the euphoria that was experienced with the first uses. During this stage it is not uncommon for the user to establish a behavioral pattern that includes missed days of work or school, being late for appointments as well as school and work, not heeding warnings about failing classes or being fired for repeated infractions, continuing to use cocaine or crack, attending parties only if crack or cocaine will be available, unexplained personality changes, and a constant need to get money to pay for his or her habit. This last problem often causes the user to turn to criminal activities that will assure a regular inflow of cash to support the habit. Robbery, theft, shoplifting, forgery, passing bad checks, and any number of other crimes are often committed without any concern for the consequences.

The first stage of withdrawal is known as craving. This causes the user to become obsessed with obtaining and using cocaine again. If the individual chooses to stop using the drug, this stage lasts approximately a week. At this point, the body no longer has a physical craving for cocaine. However, the mental obsession to use cocaine continues for a variable period of time depending on the user. He or she must work very hard to overcome this obsession or the addiction will continue, particularly because cocaine is considered to be the most potent stimulant of natural origin.[5] Situations that were associated with cocaine or crack use may easily stimulate a stronger feeling of craving. For example, people with whom the person used to get high or locations where he or she used to get high fall into this category. This is where counseling becomes an extremely important intervention, in conjunction with antidepressants.

The next stage of withdrawal causes the user to yearn for sleep. He or she will spend an inordinate amount of time thinking about sleeping because the stimulatory effects of cocaine are no longer being experienced and the nervous system is not getting the stimulation that it was experiencing during cocaine or crack use. It is not uncommon to experience depression as well for the same reason. During this stage, however, the user feels less craving for the drug. This stage may last for one to 10 weeks depending on the individual and the degree of use the person was accustomed to. It is in this stage when the user may enter a state called **anhedonia**. In this state the individual can no longer derive pleasure from experiences or activities that were once enjoyable.

The last phase of withdrawal is **extinction**. This phase often begins approximately two weeks after the user stops using cocaine or crack. Of course, this is also variable. The individual returns to a reasonably normal mood but still experiences occasional mild cravings for the cocaine or the crack. Because of this continued low-level craving, relapses into drug use are not uncommon.

Because crack cocaine exerts its effects more rapidly than powdered cocaine, the symptoms of withdrawal are somewhat more intense and include depression, anorexia, fatigue, insomnia, strong craving, shaking, irritability, anxiety, and psychiatric disturbances. At present, there are no drugs approved for replacement pharmacotherapy for cocaine or crack addiction, as **metha-**

done is used for heroin addiction. This makes withdrawal that much harder to cope with.

ADDICTION IS A CHRONIC ILLNESS

It is important to remember that addiction to cocaine and/or crack is an illness just like Alzheimer's disease, schizophrenia, depression, cardiovascular disease, and many others. It shares many features with other chronic illnesses, such as an onset and course that is directly influenced by various behaviors and environmental situations, a tendency to run in families, and the possibility that it may respond to relevant treatment.[6]

The word *chronic* is derived from the Greek word **khronikos** and the Latin word **chronicus**, both of which mean "of time." This indicates that diseases of this nature are not acute—they come on slowly and disappear in the same way. Conditions that fall into this classification take some time to develop and take a long time to disappear, if they do at all. That is why drug addiction is grouped together with the conditions listed above.

As with any chronic illness, treatment is an ongoing process and may or may not bring about the disappearance of the condition. If the disease cannot be eliminated, it is hoped that it can be reduced to a level where the patient is able to function as closely to normal as possible. Indeed, there are many cases where an individual is able to overcome his or her addiction to cocaine or crack and live a normal life. Unfortunately, there are also those who, no matter how hard and how many times they try, cannot beat the addiction permanently.

CONSEQUENCES OF COCAINE AND CRACK USE AND ADDICTION

In addition to the direct effects that cocaine and crack have on the nervous system, the rest of the body is also affected by their use. Immediate responses to the drugs' use include an increase in body temperature, heart rate, and blood pressure. Blood vessels become constricted and the pupils dilate. It is not uncommon for the user to experience headaches as well as abdominal

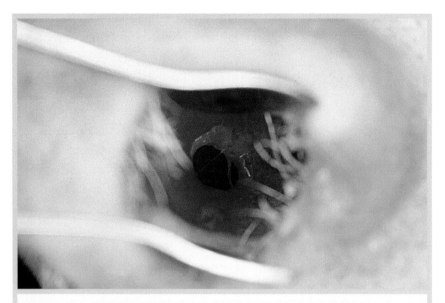

Figure 4.2 Septal perforation, a hole in the thin cartilage wall separating the nostrils of the nose, may result from chronic abuse of cocaine. *(© Dr. P. Marazzi / Photo Researchers, Inc.)*

pains and nausea. Cocaine and crack's ability to reduce the appetite often leads to the individual becoming malnourished.

The route of administration also plays a role in how the body is affected by cocaine and crack use. Those who snort cocaine frequently develop nosebleeds, a runny nose, and a loss of their sense of smell due to damage to the nasal passages. In addition, perforation of the **nasal septum** (Figure 4.2), the mucous membrane–covered bony partition that divides the nasal cavity into a left and right half, may occur, possibly leading to a collapsed nose. As the powder works its way more deeply into the respiratory tract, users will also experience hoarseness and difficulty swallowing, once again due to irritation.

Ingestion of cocaine often leads to severe bowel **gangrene** directly related to the vasoconstriction caused by cocaine. The reduction of a blood supply to the large intestine causes the tissues to become damaged and **necrotic**. Bacteria present in the colon are then able to infect the tissue and bring about the gangrene.

Intravenous use of cocaine is accompanied by severe allergic reactions both at the site of injection and systemically. These reactions may be triggered by the cocaine itself, or by one of the additives used to "cut" the cocaine. In addition, the risk of contracting blood-borne diseases such as HIV infection and hepatitis increases dramatically as many users are not careful about sharing needles with other addicts. These needles are rarely sterilized after one user injects him- or herself, and these viral diseases are easily transmitted from the blood of the first user to that of the second.

Smoking crack, besides causing the problems discussed above, also has a direct effect on the lungs. It has been long recognized that many crack smokers land in emergency rooms with symptoms that resemble pneumonia, but the condition does not respond to the antibiotics generally administered for this disease. This is because the pneumonia is not caused by any microorganisms. Instead, it is the direct effect of irritation brought about by smoking the crack. This is referred to as **crack lung**.[7] The problem is caused by inflammation of the lung tissue due to irritation from the smoke. **Corticosteroids** and **anti-inflammatory drugs** must be administered to successfully treat the condition. This response is so serious that users may experience severe bleeding from the lungs, severe chest pains, difficulty breathing, and even death from lack of oxygen or blood loss. Scarring and permanent damage to the lungs are often the results of smoking crack. Figure 4.1 shows how cocaine and crack affect the various systems of the body.

Another consequence of smoking crack is the transmission of diseases by sharing a crack pipe with another user. Pipes are often shared without regard for sterilizing the mouthpiece. In fact, tuberculosis has been shown to be transmitted through the use of a crack pipe.

The crack pipe is also the source of another problem, directly related to the heat generated by burning of the crack. The melting point of crack is 194°F (90°C) and because the smoke loses its potency quickly, crack pipes must be short so it gets into the lungs rapidly before it loses potency. This brings the lips in close contact to the crack burning in the bowl of the pipe. The result is blistered and cracked lips known as **crack lip**.

Deaths associated with cocaine and crack use are not uncommon. In addition to those deaths associated with lung damage due to crack smoking, overdoses of both cocaine and crack, and deaths due to secondary infections relating to intravenous cocaine use, death is often the result of **cardiac arrest** or a **seizure** resulting in **respiratory arrest**. One of the most common causes of cardiac arrest is the high blood pressure (hypertension) caused by the systemic vasoconstriction brought about by cocaine.

There are a number of psychological effects associated with the use of cocaine and crack as well. In addition to those changes associated with cocaine and crack use already described, there are several detrimental occurrences that are seen repeatedly in emergency rooms. One very interesting condition is **delusional parasitosis**. Users begin to believe that they are infected with parasites and actually feel parasites crawling under their skin. This sensation is called **formication**, as it feels like ants crawling under the skin (ants belong to the family *Formicidae*). These sensations are often called **cocaine bugs** or coke bugs.

Binge usage of cocaine and crack, where the individual uses the drug repeatedly and at increasing dosages, often leads to irritability, restlessness, anxiety, and **paranoia**.[8] He or she may not sleep for several days. From here the user may develop a full-blown paranoid psychosis accompanied by a loss of touch with reality and auditory hallucinations.

The use of crack and cocaine has also been linked to an increased risk of developing sexually transmitted diseases (STDs).[9] Because cocaine is purported to increase the intensity of orgasms, users tend to have sex more often and frequently practice unprotected sex, which increases the transmission of STDs. Secondly, prostitutes often use cocaine, perhaps to help them avoid thinking about the situation they are in and to help reinforce the "partying" experience they are trying to sell along with their services. STD transmission is frequently associated with prostitution. In addition, many compulsive crack and cocaine users have spent so much money on the drugs that they have no means of obtaining money other than selling sexual services. Many addicts who are suffering from clinical depression and low self-esteem are indifferent to their own health and often lack the inclination to use condoms or frequently do not have the money to pay for them. All of these factors in combination with the fact that continued use of crack and cocaine weakens the immune system help to increase the spread of STDs.

Unfortunately, many female crack and cocaine addicts do not practice safe sex techniques. One result is unwanted pregnancies. Because these women are addicted, it is impossible for most of them to stop using crack and cocaine during the pregnancy, thus causing harm to the developing fetus.

A baby born to a mother who used crack cocaine during her pregnancy is referred to as a **crack baby**. Interestingly, scientists cannot agree on whether using cocaine during a pregnancy has similar effects on the developing fetus. Researchers are beginning to follow the lives of crack babies to determine whether the concern that they will be plagued by developmental and physical ailments is legitimate.[10] Many of these researchers are claiming that the long-term effects of prenatal exposure to crack and cocaine are relatively small. Barry M. Lester, a psychiatrist at Brown University, feels that crack babies consistently show certain changes associated with maternal prenatal use of the drugs, but these effects on the brain and behavior are relatively small.

Cocaine slows fetal growth, and children born to mothers who used crack and cocaine during pregnancy tend to be smaller at birth with smaller heads than children born to mothers who did not use drugs. However, according to Deborah A. Frank, a pediatrician at Boston University, as the children grow, their brain and body size catch up.[11]

At a conference in November 2009, Lester presented an analysis of a study performed on more than 4,000 cocaine-exposed children ranging in age from four to 13. The study failed to show a statistically significant effect on I.Q. scores or language development compared to children whose mothers never used the drugs.[12]

In tests that measure specific brain functions, there is evidence that cocaine-exposed children are more likely than others to have difficulty with tasks that require visual attention and "executive function"—the brain's ability to set priorities and pay selective attention, enabling the child to focus on the task at hand. Cocaine exposure may also increase the frequency of defiant behavior and poor conduct, according to Lester's analysis. There is also some evidence that boys may be more vulnerable than girls to behavior problems.[13]

But experts say these findings are quite subtle and hard to generalize. "Just because it is statistically significant does not mean that it is a huge public health impact," said Harolyn M. Belcher, a neurodevelopmental pediatrician who is director of research at the Kennedy Krieger Institute's Family Center in Baltimore.[14]

Nevertheless, the National Institute on Drug Abuse is clear about the avoidance of cocaine and crack during pregnancy:[15]

> Many recall that "crack babies," or babies born to mothers who used crack cocaine while pregnant, were at one time written off by many as a lost generation. They were predicted to suffer from severe, irreversible damage, including reduced intelligence and social skills. It was later found that this was a gross exaggeration. However, the fact that most of these children appear normal should not be overinterpreted as indicating that there is no cause for concern. Using sophisticated technologies, scientists are now finding that exposure to cocaine during fetal development may lead to subtle, yet significant, later deficits in some children, including deficits in some aspects of cognitive performance, information-processing, and attention to tasks—abilities that are important for success in school.

It should be kept in mind as well that babies born to mothers who regularly used cocaine or crack during the pregnancy will suffer from withdrawal symptoms when they are born. This is because their supply is cut off abruptly when they are no longer connected to the mother's blood supply through the umbilical cord. They are, as the term is used, going "cold turkey." This is very difficult on the newborn and requires extensive treatment on the part of the medical staff.

Crack and cocaine use during pregnancy is not the only way that drug use may affect a child. Mothers who are breast-feeding also pose a risk to the babies. The March of Dimes issued a powerful statement in an effort to deter pregnant and nursing mothers from using cocaine, and, indirectly, crack:[16]

> Cocaine use during pregnancy can affect a pregnant woman and her unborn baby in many ways. During the early months of pregnancy, it may increase the risk of miscarriage. Later in pregnancy, it can trig-

ger preterm labor (labor that occurs before 37 weeks of pregnancy) or cause the baby to grow poorly. As a result, cocaine-exposed babies are more likely than unexposed babies to be born with low birthweight (less than 5.5 lb/2.5 kg). Low-birthweight babies are 20 times more likely to die in their first month of life than normal-weight babies, and face an increased risk of lifelong disabilities such as mental retardation and cerebral palsy. Cocaine-exposed babies also tend to have smaller heads, which generally reflect smaller brains. Some studies suggest that cocaine-exposed babies are at increased risk of birth defects, including urinary-tract defects and, possibly, heart defects. Cocaine also may cause an unborn baby to have a stroke, irreversible brain damage, or a heart attack.

5
Treatment for Cocaine and Crack Addiction

Marty told himself that he would go to the party on Saturday night even though he had to be at work on Sunday morning no later than nine o'clock. This wasn't the first time he had made this decision, even though the results the next morning were always the same. He figured he was young, healthy, and deserved to enjoy himself and would have no trouble partying, smoking crack, possibly having a few beers, and getting to work on time in the morning.

The party went exactly as he had anticipated. Marty had a good time with his friends, smoked three or four crack pipes throughout the night and felt alert, animated, and invincible. He stayed until about two in the morning and went home to get some sleep so he could go to work in the morning. He knew that if he didn't go in, he would not be paid for the day and he definitely needed the money.

Unfortunately, Marty had a great deal of difficulty getting to sleep when he arrived home thanks to the effects of the crack he had smoked and he didn't doze off until four in the morning. When his alarm went off at seven-thirty, he was so exhausted and depressed due to his crack letdown that he couldn't even get out of bed, let alone go to work. He fell back to sleep without even calling to say he wouldn't be in. Now he would lose the entire day's pay and possibly even his job. He needed the money to support himself and his crack habit. If he lost his job, his whole life would certainly change for the worse. When he took some time to think about the seriousness of the situation, he realized that it was time to get professional help for his addiction.

Marty's situation is not uncommon among cocaine and crack users and, particularly, addicts. Because of the extreme highs brought about by using cocaine and crack, followed by the "crash" that occurs when the user stops using the drugs, he or she often finds it almost impossible to get out of bed, off the couch, or off the floor for some time. This makes doing virtually anything almost impossible, including getting to work on time, or at all.

More than 70% of substance abusers are employed. The burden on employers is far-reaching and affects several areas. For example, substance abusers' medical expenses are four times greater than those of non-abusers, causing insurance carriers to raise premiums to employers who provide medical coverage for their employees. Another extra cost to employers is related to substance abusers' ability to perform. They are four times more likely to be in a workplace accident and five times more likely to file for workers' compensation. An abuser is three times more likely to be late for work and 10 times more likely to skip work altogether. What does this translate to in the dollar expense to employers? It is estimated that loss of productivity due to substance abuse totals more than $70 billion annually in the United States alone. And, just to add a further expense to the already strained finances of the employer, 25 percent of abusers steal from their employers. How do cocaine and crack users fit into all of these statistics? More than 20 million Americans use cocaine, thus placing a financial and productivity burden on millions of employers.[1]

THE ECONOMIC COSTS OF COCAINE AND CRACK ADDICTION

No price can be put on the human suffering associated with a loved one who is addicted to crack or cocaine. No cost can be put on the anguish suffered by an individual addicted to cocaine or crack. However, from a societal point of view, there are a number of costs that are borne by society when crack and cocaine addiction are involved.

Many different factors affect the costs associated with cocaine and crack addiction. Expenses for health care, lost productivity, law enforcement, incarceration, court costs, and insurance payouts are only a few.

Dr. Nora Volkow, director of the National Institute on Drug Abuse (NIDA), reported to Congress on March 1, 2007, that approximately half a trillion dollars each year is spent on health care costs, costs related to crime, and money lost due to reduced productivity when it comes to drug addiction in general. Twenty-five percent of each Medicare dollar and almost 20 percent of each Medicaid dollar are spent on drug addiction-related conditions or illnesses. Seventy percent of inmates in state prisons have used illegal drugs regularly. Drug offenders account for more than one-third of the growth in the state prison population and more than 80 percent of the increase in the number of inmates since 1985. The economic impact on the United States for addiction is twice that of any other disease that affects the brain, including Alzheimer's disease and others.[2]

In a study conducted in England, a source of great expense was uncovered that might have been overlooked in the past. Out of 1,058 participants in the survey, 36 percent reported an injection site infection within the previous year associated with injecting cocaine. The most likely user to develop an infection was a female aged 24 or older who had injected crack cocaine into the legs, groin, or hands on 14 or more days during the previous four weeks. These people tended to clean their needles and syringes for reuse. Of the 36 percent reporting an infection, two-thirds of them sought medical advice, half went to an emergency room and three-quarters ended up with a hospital admission. Conservative estimates for health care costs associated with these infections ranged from £15.5 million per year to as high as £30 million. Less conservative cost estimates suggested a maximum of £47 million or $67.5 million per year. The majority of the costs were related to hospital admissions.[3] The incidence of recent or current infections such as **cellulitis**, an infected ulcer, or an **abscess** among intravenous drug users in the United States is reported to occur in one out of three users.[4]

Another expense associated with the use of crack and cocaine is that relating to neonatal care of the newborn whose mother used drugs during pregnancy. Studies have shown that cocaine-exposed infants born to women who predominantly used crack cocaine during pregnancy had an increased length of stay in hospitals after delivery and hospital charges were more than two times that of the non-exposed group.[5] Another study showed that the average annual cost for special education for children with prenatal cocaine exposure was $6,335 per child.[6]

One might ask, "How much will a drug addict cost a nation in his or her lifetime?" This question was answered by a study conducted in Great Britain by consultants PricewaterhouseCoopers in 2008. They determined that a drug addict will cost Britain £833,000 in his or her lifetime, or roughly $1.2 million. This expense includes costs for health care, the criminal justice system, loss of earnings and productivity, and costs related to putting children into care. Male drug addicts will cost an average of £827,000 ($1.19 million) and female addicts will cost an average of £859,000 ($1.24 million). The reason for the difference is that the children of women addicts often must be taken into care because they are unable to care for them on their own. The report indicated that most of the addicts in Great Britain are addicted to crack cocaine or heroin.[7]

THE NEED FOR TREATMENT

In light of these staggering statisitics, the need for treatment of cocaine and crack addiction becomes patently obvious. Treatment comes in many forms and will vary depending on whether the patient is in an immediate crisis and requires emergency treatment, or, as in Marty's case, the individual is addicted and will require long-term treatment to cease the addictive behavior.

Cocaine and crack addiction are very complex, and are associated with intense and sometimes uncontrollable craving for the drugs, so treatment must be customized to meet the user's needs. Even though, in most cases, the path to addiction begins with the voluntary taking of crack and/or cocaine, eventually, once addiction has developed, the user no longer has the ability to stop. In addition, treatment is not simple because of the far-reaching effects that addiction has on so many aspects of the user's life.[8]

Addiction treatment must help the individual stop using drugs, maintain a drug-free lifestyle, and function productively in the family, at work, and in society. Because addiction is typically a chronic disease, people cannot simply stop using drugs for a few days and be cured. Most patients require long-term or repeated episodes of care to achieve the ultimate goal of sustained abstinence and recovery of their lives.

According to the Substance Abuse and Mental Health Services Administration's (SAMHSA) National Survey on Drug Use and Health (NSDUH), 23.2 million persons (9.4 percent of the U.S. population) aged 12 or older

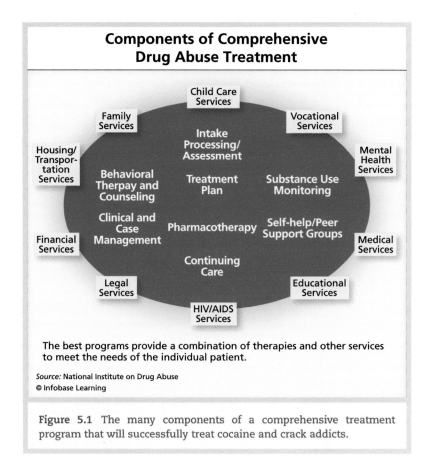

Components of Comprehensive Drug Abuse Treatment

Child Care Services

Family Services

Intake Processing/ Assessment

Vocational Services

Housing/ Transpor- tation Services

Mental Health Services

Behavioral Therpay and Counseling

Treatment Plan

Substance Use Monitoring

Clinical and Case Management

Pharmacotherapy

Self-help/Peer Support Groups

Financial Services

Medical Services

Continuing Care

Legal Services

Educational Services

HIV/AIDS Services

The best programs provide a combination of therapies and other services to meet the needs of the individual patient.

Source: National Institute on Drug Abuse
© Infobase Learning

Figure 5.1 The many components of a comprehensive treatment program that will successfully treat cocaine and crack addicts.

needed treatment for an illicit-drug or alcohol use problem in 2007. Of these individuals, 2.4 million (10.4 percent of those who needed treatment) received treatment at a specialty facility such as a hospital, drug or alcohol rehabilitation facility, or mental health center. Thus, 20.8 million persons (8.4 percent of the population aged 12 or older) needed treatment for an illicit-drug or alcohol use problem but did not receive it.[9]

PRINCIPLES OF EFFECTIVE TREATMENT

Scientific research since the mid-1970s shows that treatment can help drug-addicted patients stop using, avoid relapse, and successfully recover their lives. Based on this research, NIDA has developed a strategy that includes key principles that should form the basis of any effective treatment program:

- Addiction is a complex but treatable disease that affects brain function and behavior.
- No single treatment is appropriate for everyone.
- Treatment must be readily available.
- Effective treatment attends to multiple needs of the individual, not just his or her drug abuse.
- Remaining in treatment for an adequate period of time is critical.
- Counseling—individual and/or group—and other behavioral therapies are the most commonly used forms of drug abuse treatment.
- Medications are an important element of treatment for many patients, especially when combined with counseling and other behavioral therapies.
- An individual's treatment and services plan must be assessed continually and modified as necessary to ensure that it meets his or her changing needs.
- Many drug-addicted individuals also have other mental disorders.
- Medically assisted detoxification is only the first stage of addiction treatment and by itself does little to change long-term drug abuse.
- Treatment does not need to be voluntary to be effective.
- Drug use during treatment must be monitored continuously, as lapses during treatment do occur.
- Treatment programs should assess patients for the presence of HIV/AIDS, hepatitis B and C, tuberculosis, and other infectious diseases, as well as provide targeted risk-reduction counseling to help patients modify or change behaviors that place them at risk of contracting or spreading infectious diseases.

APPROACHES TO EFFECTIVE TREATMENT

In order to treat a cocaine or crack addict effectively, the first step is to detoxify the patient. This requires that the individual stop using crack and cocaine. Of course, this leads to withdrawal, which must be treated with supportive medications that suppress it and reverse the symptoms. For example, the severe depression that occurs may be treated with antidepressant medications. Unfortunately, there are no currently available drugs for reestablishing normal brain function, diminishing cravings, and preventing relapses following cocaine and crack cessation. There are medications that will treat heroin, morphine, tobacco, and alcohol addictions, and much research is being done on new medicines to treat cocaine and crack addicts.

In addition to medication, behavioral therapy performed by qualified psychologists, psychiatrists, drug counselors, and clinical social workers is of great importance, particularly in light of the fact that specific medications are not yet available. These therapies could include cognitive-behavioral therapy (used to help patients recognize, avoid, and cope with situations that would cause them to use the drugs), motivational interviewing (used in patients who are ready, willing, and able to change their behavior), motivational incentives (in which positive reinforcement is used to encourage abstinence from drug use), and multidimensional family therapy (developed for adolescents with drug abuse problems and their families in order to improve family functioning).

EMERGENCY CARE

In cases of cocaine overdose, special emergency measures must be taken if the patient is to survive. Initially, emergency room staff must be sure that the patient's airway is unobstructed and that he or she is able to take in sufficient oxygen. Monitoring of cardiac function is essential at this point. The patient's body temperature may rise and must be brought down to normal levels.

In cases where the patient has overdosed on inhaled cocaine powder, it is important to examine the nostrils and remove any residue of cocaine powder as this will continue to have an affect on the individual.

In order to calm the patient down if he or she is extremely agitated, or to slow down the rapid heart rate and lower the high blood pressure that often accompanies cocaine overdose, restraints are generally not recommended because they often make the patient even more agitated. Instead, it is recommended that an antianxiety drug such as benzodiazepine (Valium) be administered. Experience with this drug in these situations has proven it to be safe and effective. Also, because the effects of cocaine overdose or heavy usage are short lived, monitoring of the user is an excellent tool in determining when he or she is ready to start discussing a long-term solution to the problem.

REHABILITATION AND THERAPY

Treating a patient for cocaine or crack addiction may be done either on an outpatient or residential basis, based on the individual's specific wants and needs. Residential treatment is often preferable as it removes the user from the environment that is associated with the situations and temptations that brought about the addictive behavior in the first place. Patients who are in a less severe situation can do well with outpatient treatment. In either case, the longer a user stays in a treatment program, the better the outcome. In fact, people who stay active in a treatment program for 1 year or more do much better in the long run.[10]

At the present time there is no medication to treat cocaine and crack addiction. Much research is being done along those lines and there is hope that soon a specific medicine will be developed. An older medication that has shown promise but is not yet approved by the U.S. Food and Drug Administration (FDA) to treat cocaine and crack addiction is disulfiram (Antabuse). This drug is approved by the FDA to help alcoholics stop drinking. When disulfiram is taken with alcohol or cocaine, the user becomes violently ill. Symptoms include accelerated heart rate, shortness of breath, nausea, vomiting, a throbbing headache, and, possibly, fainting. These uncomfortable symptoms become associated with the drug use and help the addict modify his or her behavior to avoid using them.

In the absence of a drug that directly treats cocaine and crack addiction, a sound therapy program will begin with detoxification of the patient. During this phase the patient's body is cleared of cocaine and any toxins and chemicals produced by the drug. The process is uncomfortable as the user continues to crave the cocaine. Nevertheless, it is an important first step in a successful treatment process.[11]

Following detoxification, it is important to address any physical ailments that the user has. In addition, the physician or team must provide the patient with tools for recovery. Relaxing activities such as walks on the beach, meditation, listening to music, yoga, or any other undertaking that will calm the user are a good way to move into the next phase of therapy.

Figure 5.2 Behavioral therapy is one aspect of treatment for those with drug abuse problems. *(National Institute of Mental Health)*

In addition, providing the patient with a well-designed meal plan also is of extreme importance. Once the physical aspects of rehabilitation are attended to, the patient may move into the phase where the emotional and mental issues are addressed. This is where the many forms of counseling cited above may be employed.

DRUG REHABILITATION PROGRAMS

There are many programs that treat cocaine and crack addicts. The abundance of these programs can make it difficult for the addict to decide which one will provide the best therapy. The right drug rehabilitation program must provide several options for treatment. The facility should have inpatient, short-stay, outpatient, and residential options so that different needs may be met. The length of stay in an inpatient or residential program is determined by the severity and stage of the addiction.

Because cocaine and crack addiction affect not only the addict but his or her family as well, the choice of which rehabilitation program to enter must also be made after finding out how much of the therapy will involve family members. If a program offers only a few lecture sessions and does not deal directly with each of the family members, it will not be as effective as one that includes individual and family group counseling sessions.

Recovery from addiction is an ongoing process. Therefore, it is crucial that the rehabilitation program includes numerous follow-up visits during which the user's recovery is closely monitored and supported. This follow-up care will help the addict to incorporate the skills learned during intensive treatment into everyday life.

The U.S. Department of Health and Human Services, through SAMHSA, provides an extensive list of substance abuse treatment facilities on its Web site that enables the user to find programs in every state.[12] Detailed maps are provided for each facility listed along with the address and phone number. This free service may be extremely helpful for an addict who is attempting to straighten out his or her life.

TREATMENT WHEN MONEY IS A PROBLEM

The cost of treating a cocaine or crack addict is quite expensive. Many health insurance plans provide coverage for treatment programs. The limits on the maximum amount of this benefit vary from company to company and policy to policy. In addition, most facilities that offer drug addiction treatment programs provide a sliding scale of payments based on the patient's financial situation.

Nevertheless, there are many addicts who are unable to afford to pay anything for their treatment. Often this is directly related to the high cost of maintaining their habits. In these situations there are programs available that are paid for with public funds. Once again, SAMHSA provides information online to direct individuals to state substance abuse agencies where they will receive information on free treatment programs in their areas.[13] The list is alphabetized by state and U.S. territory to make finding the agency easy for the addict or his or her family. For individuals who do not have computer access, toll-free phone numbers are provided (1-800-662-HELP, 1-800-662-9832 [in Spanish], 1-800-228-0427 [hearing impaired]).

HOW EFFECTIVE ARE TREATMENT PROGRAMS?

The effectiveness of a treatment program depends on many factors including the patient's willingness to beat the addiction, the type of program provided, the length of the program, the addict's support system, and many other elements. The length of programs may range from two weeks to two years. The shorter programs are usually done as a 12-step inpatient or outpatient model and have a success rate of only 3 percent to 18 percent.[14] Longer programs that include constant follow-up and counseling show higher rates of success. Some claim to be 75 percent successful.[15]

6

Cocaine, Crack, and the Law

Money was very tight and Sally knew that she had to come up with some means of making it so she could pay her rent, her telephone bill, buy gas for her car, and handle other bills that had to be taken care of. Sally had been using crack cocaine on and off for several years. She had never gotten caught by the authorities and wasn't truly addicted to it, although she certainly did get cravings for it from time to time between uses. She realized that she might be able to put her drug connection to good use by purchasing some crack at a reduced price from one of her suppliers from her old neighborhood and selling it on the streets of the poor neighborhood where she now lived. The profit would more than cover her financial needs.

She went back to where she used to live, found her contact, and made a sizeable purchase of crack. As she knew many addicts in her new neighborhood, she was sure there would be no problem finding buyers for her product. Sally made many sales that day to various addicts that she was familiar with. As nightfall approached, she made one more sale to a middle-aged man whom she hadn't seen before, but who looked like he was addicted. That was her big mistake.

The new "customer" turned out to be an undercover detective assigned to the narcotics bureau of the police department. He arrested her on the spot for possession of a sizeable quantity of crack cocaine and for selling it, both felonies.

Her public defender did her best to get a minimal sentence for Sally's offense. After all, she didn't have a criminal record and, although she used crack repeatedly, she had never been caught. However, the judge sentenced Sally to 10 years in the state prison followed by three years' probation after her eventual release.

For hundreds of years, laws have been passed aimed at limiting the consumption of foods, beverages, and drugs. These laws, known as sumptuary laws, were passed in an effort to help the privileged class retain its elevated position in relation to the peasants. Limits were placed on how much of a particular commodity could be consumed. In truth, they were not very effective.[1]

Clearly, many drugs are readily available to the public without restrictions. These over-the-counter drugs include common pharmaceuticals like aspirin, several antihistamines, cough medicines, nasal sprays, and numerous others. Some, such as a few cold remedies, have their sales recorded so that a record may be kept to determine whether an individual is purchasing an excessive amount that may indicate a substance abuse problem. Still others are restricted to sale by a licensed pharmacist only on the order of a physician with a valid prescription, which helps governments regulate the sale, manufacture, and distribution of specific medications.

Many restricted drugs, such as antidepressants, antianxiety drugs, painkillers, and other psychoactive drugs have found a large market through illegal trade. Because of their effects on an individual's personality, these drugs are widely sought after by people of all ages who cannot get a legitimate prescription from a physician. This creates a widespread **black market** for these medications.

In the United States a prohibition was placed on cocaine in the early part of the twentieth century. Much of this was fueled, not by the government's concern for the detrimental effects of the drug, but by racism. It was believed that white women would be attacked by black men high on cocaine.[2] In 1910 Dr. Hamilton Wright, the U.S. Opium Commissioner, reported that construction contractors would provide cocaine to their black laborers in order to make them more productive.[3]

Within a few years this sort of racially motivated misinformation grew. An article in the *New York Times* in 1914 claimed that most attacks on white women in the South were carried out by "cocaine-crazed" black men.[4] According to the writer, Dr. E. H. Williams, restrictions imposed by the white legislature in the South on the use of alcohol by blacks was causing them to resort to sniffing cocaine in order to get high. To substantiate his claim, Dr. Williams compared the rate of increase in cocaine use in Raleigh, North Carolina, and Knoxville and Memphis, Tennessee. He claimed that in the first two cities, where a prohibition on the sale of alcohol to blacks was strictly enforced, the use of cocaine doubled within a four-year period. In Memphis, where this prohibition was not in place, the amount of cocaine use was increasing slowly, if at all.[5]

In an effort to curb the sale and use of drugs of addiction, the Harrison Narcotics Tax Act was passed by Congress. It was proposed by Representative Francis Burton Harrison of New York and approved on December 17, 1914. U.S. Opium Commissioner Wright was instrumental in drafting the act. It was described as: "An Act to provide for the registration of, with collectors of internal revenue, and to impose a special tax on all persons who produce, import, manufacture, compound, deal in, dispense, sell, distribute, or give away opium or coca leaves, their salts, derivatives, or preparations, and for other purposes."[6]

Many antidrug laws have been enacted throughout the United States on both the federal and state level. The Controlled Substances Act was passed into law on October 27, 1970, by Congress as Title II of the Comprehensive Drug Abuse Prevention and Control Act of 1970. More specifically, it is Title 21, Chapter 13, Subchapter 1 of the act that addresses drug abuse prevention and control. This act addresses not only the control of illegal substances but also those that are prescribed by physicians, so that they are not used illegally. The control includes transport both within and between U.S. states and that to and from other countries.[7]

Congress made the following findings and declarations:

- Many of the drugs included within this subchapter have a useful and legitimate medical purpose and are necessary to maintain the health and general welfare of the American people.
- The illegal importation, manufacture, distribution, and possession and improper use of controlled substances have a substantial and detrimental effect on the health and general welfare of the American people.
- A major portion of the traffic in controlled substances flows through interstate and foreign commerce. Incidents of the traffic which are not an integral part of the interstate or foreign flow also have a substantial and direct effect upon interstate commerce.

- Local distribution and possession of controlled substances contribute to swelling the interstate traffic in such substances.
- Controlled substances manufactured and distributed interstate cannot be differentiated from controlled substances manufactured and distributed intrastate.
- Federal control of the intrastate incidents of the traffic in controlled substances is essential to the effective control of the interstate incidents of such traffic.
- The United States is a party to the Single Convention on Narcotic Drugs, 1961, and other international conventions designed to establish effective control over international and domestic traffic in controlled substances.

The act was amended 17 times between 1974 and 2009 to keep up with societal and legal changes in order to keep it current and effective. This did not change its basic intent to control the manufacture, transport, importation, exportation and illegal use of legitimate medications and illegal drugs such as cocaine and crack.

Following passage of the Harrison Act in 1914, and the development of cheaper, legal substances such as amphetamines, the use of cocaine began to diminish and it became scarce. However, in the 1960s the incidence of its use began to rise again because the middle and upper-middle class realized that the exaggerated anticocaine campaign that the government had used for three decades was not truthful. This resurgence of cocaine use prompted cocaine's classification in 1970 by Congress as a Schedule II substance.[8]

INDIVIDUAL STATE LAWS VARY

In addition to federal regulations regarding crack and cocaine, each state has its own set of rules governing the possession, use, sale, and trafficking of cocaine and crack. Some states' penalties are much harsher than others. In the end, sale, use, possession, and trafficking will most likely put the perpetrator in jail.

A quick comparison of the five randomly selected states profiled in Table 6.1 shows that laws vary from state to state. Fines are different and penalties may be increased several-fold when drug sales take place on school

Table 6.1 Comparison of Some States' Laws Governing Cocaine	
California	
Code Section	Health & Safety §11000, et seq. §11350, et seq.
Possession	State prison and fine up to $70; if probation granted, there are additional requirements
Sale	State prison 2–4 yrs.; Possession or sale of "cocaine base": state prison 3–5 yrs.; Sale to minors: state prison 3, 5, or 7 yrs.; Sale to day care, preschool, or school children: 5, 7, or 9 yrs.; Anyone over 18 who sells to a minor or uses a minor in the sale process is punishable in state prison for 3, 6, or 9 yrs.; Sale within 1000 ft. of school: additional 3, 4, or 5 yrs.; If sale occurred upon the grounds of a child day care, school, church, synagogue, or youth center, punishment is automatically enhanced by one year; Anyone over 18 yrs who sells to a minor at least 4 years younger as a full and separate enhancement shall be punished by imprisonment in state prison for 3, 4, or 5 yrs. Sale on many public areas punishable by state prison for 5, 7, or 9 yrs. if seller 5 yrs. older than minor
Trafficking	Transport/import 3–5 yrs.; County to noncontiguous county: 3, 6, or 9 yrs.
New York	
Code Section	Penal §§220, et seq.; Pub. Health §§3306, 3307
Possession	Knowingly possessing: Any amount: Class A misdemeanor; Criminal possession in the fifth (5th) degree Over 500 mg.: Class D felony; Over 2 oz.: Class A-II felony; Over 4 oz.: class A-I felony; Any amount with intent to sell: Class D felony; Any amount of narcotic drug with intent to sell: Class B felony
Sale	Class D felony in general, then: Over 2 oz.: Class A-I felony; On school grounds or narcotic preparation to someone under 21: Class B felony
Trafficking	---------
Florida	
Code Section	775.082 to 775.084; 893.01, et seq.
Possession	3rd degree felony; Possession of 28 g is trafficking (1st degree felony)

(continues)

Table 6.1 (*continued*)	
Sale	2nd degree felony (penalties more severe near school)
Trafficking	All sentencing is to be done pursuant to sentencing guidelines: 28–200 g: $50,000 and 3 yrs.; 200–400 g.: $100,000 and 7 yrs.; 400 g.–150 kg.: 15 yrs. and $250,000; Over 150 kg.: 1st degree felony with life imprisonment
Colorado	
Code Section	18–18–101, et seq. 18–18–405
Sale	Class 4 felony; Subsequent Offense: twice or more within 6 months and amount greater than 28.5 g: Defendant shall be sentenced to the Dept. of Corrections for at least the minimum and fined no less than $1,000 but not over $500,000 with no probation or suspension
Possession	Class 3 felony; Sale to minor within 1000 ft. of school or public property–Dept. of Corrections for minimum 5 yrs.; Subsequent offense near school: 20 yrs.
Trafficking	---------
Texas	
Code Section	Health & Safety §§481.001, et seq.
Sale	Less than 1 g: state jail felony; 1–4 g: 3rd degree felony; 4–200 g: 2nd degree felony; 200–400 g: 1st degree felony; 400 g and over: 10–99 yrs. or life at Texas Dept. of Criminal Justice institution and/or $100,000
Possession	Less than 1 g: state jail felony; 1–4 g: 2nd degree felony; 4–200 g: 1st degree felony; 200–400 g: Texas Dept. of Criminal Justice institution for life or 10–99 yrs. and/or $100,000; 400 g and over: Texas Dept. of Criminal Justice institution for life or 15–99 yrs. and/or $250,000; Delivery to minor under 17 who is enrolled in school: 2nd degree felony; Within drug-free zone: penalties doubled
Trafficking	---------

Source: FindLaw, "State Cocaine Laws," http://law.findlaw.com/state-laws/cocaine/(accessed September 29, 2010).

grounds. This is one area where most states are very protective and penalties are harsh.

As noted earlier in this book, the penalties for sale, use, and possession of crack cocaine are much harsher than those for powdered cocaine. This is true on the federal level and also at most state levels. For possession of crack cocaine, most states do not specify quantity requirements when it comes to sentencing. However, they require increased penalties for possession of 25 grams or more.[9]

In 1986, when newly enacted federal sentencing laws relating to crack cocaine went into effect, many states used these laws as a guide to determine penalties for possession of small amounts of the substance. Possession of 5 or more grams of crack required a mandatory prison term of five years. This was generally much harsher than the sentencing associated with possession of equal amounts of powdered cocaine. Between January 1, 2005, and December 31, 2007, there were more than 10,000 felony cocaine convictions resulting in federal prison terms of 10 or more years. More than 90% of these felony cases involved the sale and distribution of crack cocaine.[10]

In 2008 the U.S. Sentencing Commission (USSC), an independent agency in the judicial branch of the government, determined that prison terms for crack cocaine possession were both too long and too harsh. This brought about a small change in the sentencing laws for mandatory prison terms relating to crack cocaine possession: the mandatory prison term was once 10 years, and it was now reduced to eight.

In addition, if a first-time defendant is charged with simple possession of crack cocaine, he or she may qualify to participate in the judicial diversion process. The federal government and many states are relying on this method of dealing with crack users to help keep the already overcrowded prisons from getting worse. Judicial diversion means that instead of a case going to trial, it may be diverted from prosecution if the defendant enters a pretrial intervention program to help him or her stop using crack. To qualify for diversion, the possession charge must be the defendant's first and only serious drug offense. It does not apply if the charges include sale or distribution of crack cocaine.

The federal government is very serious about seizing illegal cocaine. It dedicates a great deal of resources to take as much of the drug off the market as possible. Figure 6.1 provides some interesting seizure statistics.

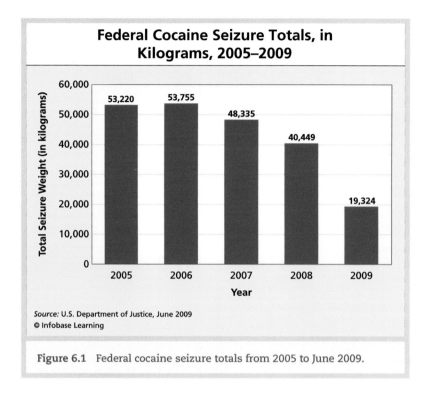

Figure 6.1   Federal cocaine seizure totals from 2005 to June 2009.

An analysis of the data in Figure 6.1 indicates that the amount of cocaine seized has declined steadily since 2007. This does not reflect a loss of interest on the part of users. Instead, there has been a shortage of cocaine. Although no single factor for the decline in cocaine availability can be identified, a combination of factors, including increased law enforcement efforts in Mexico and the transit zones, decreased cocaine production in Colombia, high levels of cartel violence, and cocaine flow to non-U.S. markets likely contributed to decreased amounts being transported to the U.S.-Mexico border for subsequent smuggling into the United States. Cocaine production estimates for Colombia decreased slightly in 2007 and significantly in 2008, reducing the amount of cocaine available to world markets. Traffickers in Bolivia and Peru produced sizable quantities of cocaine during the two-year period, but their estimated production capability and well-established trafficking networks were not able to quickly fill voids in the U.S. cocaine supply caused by the decline in Colombian production. During 2007, several exceptionally large seizures of cocaine destined for Mexico may have initiated the first reported cocaine shortages in U.S. drug markets. These seizures coincided with the decline in seizures along the southwest border of the United States and were followed by an unprecedented decline in cocaine availability, a trend that continued through 2009. Helping to sustain the shortages were counterdrug efforts on both sides of the border, which most likely diminished the ability of one or more major drug trafficking organizations to obtain cocaine from South America for subsequent distribution in the United States. Finally, expanding world markets for cocaine in Europe (a highly profitable market) and South America may be further reducing the already reduced amount available from Colombian sources to distribute in the United States.[11]

Agents of the federal government do not actively seize crack because trafficking does not actually occur. Rather, it is the cocaine that is turned into crack that is trafficked, thus, seizing it will directly reduce the amount of crack

Figure 6.2 One of the largest seizures of cocaine in U.S. history occurred in March 2007 when the DEA and U.S. Coast Guard seized 19 metric tons of cocaine from a vessel off the coast of Panama. The cocaine was headed to Mexican drug traffickers. *(U.S. Drug Enforcement Administration)*

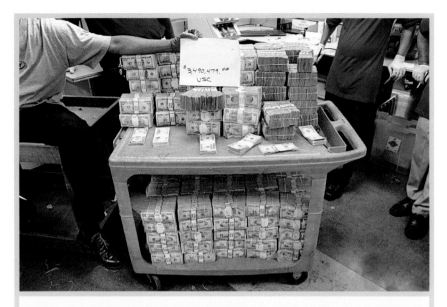

Figure 6.3 Federal authorities commonly seize large quantities of drug money during raids. Pictured is almost $3.5 million of the more than $45 million in cash seized as part of Operation Imperial Emperor in February 2007. *(U.S. Drug Enforcement Administration)*

that can be made. Both federal and local law enforcement agencies have been successful at seizing sizeable quantities of cocaine.

In addition to the DEA, the U.S. Coast Guard periodically seizes cocaine in raids on ships that are trying to import cocaine from other nations. On September 5, 2001, Operation Sanctuary, an operation carried out by the DEA in conjunction with the Dominican Republic's National Drug Control Directorate (NDCD), came to an end, having successfully achieved the seizure of 2,899 kilograms (6,551 pounds) of cocaine along with $2.5 million in U.S. currency. In addition, the operation led to arrests of 43 individuals working for a Colombian money laundering organization that operated in Colombia, New York, Miami, West Palm Beach, and San Juan, Puerto Rico.

In another very successful raid, on March 21, 2007, the Coast Guard seized 19 metric tons of cocaine (Figure 6.2). This was the largest maritime seizure of cocaine in history.

Along with cocaine, money is often seized during a raid. Over the years, hundreds of millions of dollars have been confiscated along with tons of cocaine and other drugs during raids on houses, business, ships at sea, and various other locations.

COCAINE AND CRACK USE MAY LEAD TO CRIMINAL ACTIVITIES

For any number of reasons, both use and, more commonly, addiction to cocaine and crack often lead to criminal activities. Particularly in the case of crack, because it is so often used in the ghettos by financially troubled individuals, robbery becomes a means of obtaining money to support the habit. Muggings, holdups at knife- and gunpoint, carjackings, robberies of convenience stores and gas stations, and numerous other forms of thievery are all commonly associated with addiction to cocaine and crack. In addition, drug addicts often resort to prostitution to make money to support their habits.

Table 6.2 Percent of Adult Arrestees Reporting Crack Cocaine Use, by City, 2008		
	Past 30 Day Use	Past Year Use
Atlanta, Ga.	23.4%	25.0%
Charlotte, N.C.	13.9	18.2
Chicago, Ill.	23.0	24.2
Denver, Colo.	16.7	20.3
Indianapolis, Ind.	10.6	14.2
Minneapolis, Minn.	14.7	15.5
New York, N.Y.	7.2	9.1
Portland, Ore.	10.8	16.2
Sacramento, Calif.	8.9	10.7
Washington, D.C.	17.8	17.5
Source: Office of National Drug Control Policy. "Crack Facts and Figures." http://www.whitehousedrugpolicy.gov/drugfact/crack/crack_ff.html#legislation. Accessed on June 29, 2010.		

One study showed that there was a significant positive association between crack use and the number of sexual partners, regardless of the type of sex involved.[12] Both males and females who used crack had more sexual partners for all types of sexual activities than did those who did not use crack.

Along the same lines, another study indicated that HIV infection is disproportionately high among African Americans, accounting for more than half of the new infections in the United States. The two main reasons for this are intravenous drug use and having sex with multiple partners, especially concurrently. Smoking crack is one of the most important contributing factors for this statistic because it creates a sense of euphoria and reduces sexual inhibitions. When withdrawn, the users become depressed and strongly crave more crack, leading to a powerful compulsion to obtain the drug that causes them to trade sex for crack with multiple partners, often without the use of condoms.

The Arrestee Drug Abuse Monitoring II (ADAM II) program is designed to gather information on drug use and related matters from adult male offenders within 48 hours of arrest. ADAM II serves as a critical source of data for estimating trends in drug use in local areas, understanding the relationship between drugs and crime, and describing drug market activity in the adult male arrestee population in 10 U.S. cities during 2008. Table 6.2 shows the correlation between arrestees and the percentage of drug use among them in the 10 cities included in the monitoring program.

7

Cocaine and Crack: Looking to the Future

Alexander was a very successful cocaine dealer whose clientele included many business executives and famous personalities. He was usually very careful when selling his product, but on one day he became a bit greedy and agreed to sell 500 grams of cocaine to several different, seemingly high-class buyers whom he had never met before. The "buyers" were undercover police, and Alexander was quickly arrested. Because the federal government's statutes require a minimum sentence of five years for the sale of 500 grams of cocaine, Alexander was off the streets.

At the same time, across town in the inner city, Andy was selling crack cocaine to his regular customers on the street. They were glad to see him and quick to buy what he had to sell in order to get high. Some new buyers appeared on the street and, although Andy had some doubts about the wisdom of selling to them, his desire for money helped him to overcome his fear. He sold five grams of crack cocaine to the strangers, who turned out to be undercover police officers. The police department was eager to round up drug dealers and had put many undercover officers on duty to catch them. Federal regulations require a mandatory five-year prison sentence for selling just 5 grams of crack, so Andy got the same sentence as Alexander. Clearly, there is a great incongruity in the sentencing guidelines set forth by the federal government.

THE FUTURE OF CRACK AND COCAINE LAWS

What happened in the story above happens every day in many areas of the country. The federal government's sentencing guidelines for sale of cocaine and crack differ greatly. Some see a bias in this fact, as cocaine is most often used by the upper middle class and the upper class, which consist mostly of white people, while crack cocaine is most widely used in poor areas where the majority of users (85%) are black.[1] Because many drug abuse laws date back to the Anti-Drug Abuse Acts of the 1980s, many people feel that revisions are needed to make the laws and penalties more just. This is only one of the facets associated with the future of cocaine and crack cocaine. Several bills have been placed before Congress, including H.R. 3245, the Fairness in Cocaine Sentencing Act of 2009. This act was designed to amend the Controlled Substances Act and the Controlled Substances Import and Export Act to eliminate increased and mandatory minimum drug penalties for drug offenses involving mixtures or substances that contain cocaine base, such as crack cocaine.[2]

The Senate also wrote a similar bill, S. 1789, the Fair Sentencing Act of 2010, which was signed into law by President Obama on August 3, 2010. This bill increases the amount of a controlled substance or mixture containing a cocaine base (that is, crack cocaine) required for the imposition of mandatory minimum prison terms for trafficking and increase monetary penalties for drug trafficking and for the importation and exportation of controlled substances. It also eliminated the five-year mandatory minimum prison term for first-time possession of crack cocaine.[3] This modification directly affects African Americans in poor areas who are caught using crack by lessening the harsh penalties now imposed on them, thus reducing the bias created by the current drug laws.

In addition to these changes, the law directs the U.S. Sentencing Commission to: (1) review and amend its sentencing guidelines to increase sentences for defendants convicted of using violence during a drug trafficking offense; (2) incorporate aggravating and mitigating factors in its guidelines for drug trafficking offenses; (3) promulgate guidelines, policy statements, or amendments required by this act as soon as practicable, but not later than 90 days after the enactment of this act; and (4) study and report to Congress on the impact of changes in sentencing law under this act.

During his campaign, President Obama made it clear that, if elected, he was determined to make changes in the crack/powdered cocaine sentence disparity. In April 2009 Assistant Attorney General Lanny Breuer, a member of the Obama administration, and U.S. District Judge Reggie Walton, an African American, testified before a Senate Judiciary subcommittee. Judge Walton claimed, "Jails are loaded with people who look like me," while Assistant Attorney General Breuer stated that Congress's goal "should be to completely eliminate the disparity" in sentencing. "A growing number of citizens view it as fundamentally unfair," he said.[4]

"This administration believes our criminal laws should be tough, smart, fair," Breuer said, but also should "promote public trust and confidence in the criminal justice system." Judge Walton asserted the United States was "mistaken" to enact the disparity. "There's no greater violence in cases before me," he noted. The Obama administration has said it would also like to increase the number of drug treatment programs as well as rehabilitation programs for felons after their release from prison.

The reason for the disparity that was created in 1986 is based on crack's ability to bring on a high much more quickly than cocaine and its increased risk of addiction compared to cocaine. Senator Dick Durbin (D-IL), who worked with Senate Republicans on the proposed legislation, said, "If this bill is enacted into law, it will immediately ensure that every year, thousands of people are treated more fairly in our criminal justice system." He explained why in 1986, when he was a member of the House of Representatives, he supported the bill that allowed the discrepancy. "Crack cocaine had just appeared on the scene, and it scared us because it was cheap, addictive. We thought it was more dangerous than many narcotics," he said.[5]

CLINICAL TRIALS TO FIGHT ADDICTION

Another aspect relating to cocaine and crack is how to handle addiction. Numerous clinical trials are being conducted throughout the world that address this issue. The Assistance Publique—Hôpitaux de Paris is conducting a Phase III trial to determine the efficacy of modafinil, a drug that has been approved by the FDA to treat **narcolepsy**, in treating cocaine addiction. Its mode of action appears to be to increase the neurotransmitters dopamine and norepinephrine. It also elevates histamine levels in the hypothalamus, which acts to promote wakefulness.[6]

Because cocaine blocks dopamine transporters in the synapse, resulting in powerful feelings of euphoria, and modafinil may be able to reverse these effects, the researchers are attempting to use it to treat addiction during therapeutic cocaine withdrawal (the withdrawal associated with voluntary cessation of cocaine use during addiction treatment). Some subjects will receive a placebo. All subjects will undergo positron emission tomography (PET) scans, cerebral magnetic resonance imaging (MRI), urinary toxicity screens, blood analyses, clinical scale exams for craving and depression, and neuropsychological evaluations. The estimated completion date of this study is July 2011.

Another research study being conducted is aimed at treating patients with bipolar I disorder and cocaine dependence. In this study, conducted by the University of Texas Southwestern Medical Center in collaboration with the National Institute on Drug Abuse (NIDA), citicoline (cytidine diphosphate choline), a drug that increases the density of dopamine receptors and is used to improve focus and mental energy, will be tested in conjunction with cognitive-behavioral therapy to determine whether it may be used to treat both conditions together. Once again, a placebo will also be included in the study. This clinical trial is expected to be completed by April 2012.[7]

It is not unusual to find cocaine addicts also addicted to other drugs. A research study designed to determine whether or not topiramate (Topamax), an anticonvulsant and antimigraine drug, is effective in treating cocaine addiction in opiate-dependent drug users being maintained on methadone is being conducted by Johns Hopkins University in collaboration with the NIDA. The study will determine whether topiramate may be used safely by individuals taking methadone, if it will effectively treat cocaine addiction, and if it will reduce collateral problems such as alcohol abuse, tobacco dependence, anxiety, post-traumatic stress disorder, and/or pain symptoms. A placebo control will also be used in this study.[8]

Relapses in cocaine abusers are very common, so it is extremely important to find drugs that will help the addict who is attempting to stop using the substance to avoid using it again once he or she has attempted to stop. A clinical trial sponsored by the University of Arkansas in collaboration with

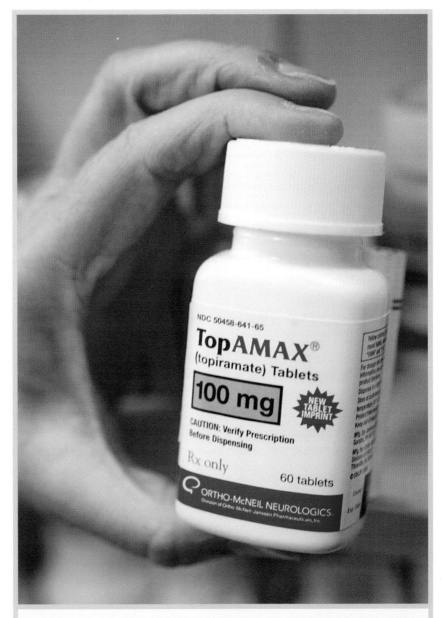

Figure 7.1 Topiramate, an anticonvulsant and antimigraine drug, is being tested for use in treating cocaine addiction. (© *Lee Powers/ Photo Researchers, Inc.*)

the NIDA is being conducted to explore a new way to extend and maintain drug abstinence in people addicted to cocaine. The researchers will combine D-cycloserine (DCS), an antibiotic used against tuberculosis bacteria when standard antibiotics are ineffective, in conjunction with cognitive-behavioral therapy to determine if test subjects are able to remain drug free for longer periods of time. DCS has been shown to enhance learning of new information, so the researchers want to use it before an addict learns new techniques to cope with the powerful drug craving associated with cocaine use. In addition, the researchers will use MRI images of the brain before and after DCS administration to identify areas of the brain that are being activated when a new technique is being learned. A placebo control for DCS will be used. The study is scheduled to be completed by May 2011.[9]

There are several hundred active clinical trials currently addressing cocaine addiction. Because the basic chemical in crack is cocaine, it is assumed that drugs useful in treating cocaine addiction will also work well in treating crack addiction.

In a different approach to understanding addiction to crack and cocaine, a study has begun that addresses the genetic background that may be linked to addiction. The Centre Hospitalier Universitaire de Fort-de-France in Martinique is conducting a study that will involve the collection of 10 milliliters of saliva from the test subjects, all men. The subjects must all be addicted to crack and must also suffer from sensation-seeking, impulsivity, and childhood attention–deficit/hyperactivity disorder (ADHD). The researchers claim to have found a link between these three behaviors and specific structures on two genes labeled DRD2 and DRD4. These genes regulate dopamine activity by coding for the production of dopamine receptors, thus providing a link to crack and cocaine addiction. A DNA extraction will be performed on the saliva so that researchers may determine the condition of these two genes in the addicts. The study is expected to be completed by December 2012.[10]

A DIFFERENT APPROACH

In October 2009, researchers developed a vaccine called TA-CD that was designed to treat cocaine and crack addiction. The concept was to allow the body's immune system to create antibodies to cocaine that would bind to the cocaine molecules, making them too large to get into the brain because they are stopped by the blood-brain barrier; thus, the substance would have no euphoric effect.[11] This is different from the process used to prevent diseases wherein antibodies act directly against the bacteria, viruses, or toxins that cause a particular disease.

Initial results showed a substantial reduction in cocaine use in 38% of vaccinated patients. "The results of this study represent a promising step toward an effective medical treatment for cocaine addiction," said NIDA director Dr. Nora Volkow. "Provided that larger follow-up studies confirm its safety and efficacy, this vaccine would offer a valuable new approach to treating cocaine addiction, for which no FDA-approved medication is currently available."[12]

The vaccine did not achieve complete abstinence from cocaine in the test subjects. Nevertheless, even a reduction in use helps the addict to function more normally, which is an improvement in quality of life. However, one response occurred that researchers did not expect: Some of the addicts in the study began using massive amounts of cocaine in an effort to overcome the effects of the vaccine. Dr. Thomas R. Kosten, a professor of psychiatry and neuroscience at Baylor College of Medicine in Houston, Texas, and the lead researcher of the study, said, "After the vaccine, doing cocaine was a very disappointing experience for them. Nobody overdosed, but some of them had 10 times more cocaine coursing through their systems than researchers had encountered before." About 25% of the test subjects did not make sufficient antibodies at all. Researchers could not explain this.[13]

In a similar study using the same vaccine, Dr. Margaret Haney, a professor of clinical neuroscience at Columbia University Medical Center, gave crack cocaine to each test subject 39 times over 13 weeks. The subjects had to fill out several surveys about their moods throughout the study. The results were surprisingly positive and Haney concluded that the vaccine could be useful to protect motivated treatment-seekers from relapses if they tried to stop and then used a small amount of cocaine. Her feeling was that the vaccine would help to curb their craving for higher doses of crack.[14]

NUCLEIC ACIDS MAY STOP ADDICTION

A recent discovery involving small fragments of **RNA** may be the answer to stopping cocaine and crack addiction in the future. Working with mice, researchers at the Scripps Research Institute in Jupiter, Florida, discovered that as mice consumed cocaine, an increase in a very small fragment of RNA known as microRNA-212 occurred. (MicroRNA is a regulatory piece of informational genome.) As they continued to consume the cocaine, their levels of microRNA-212 continued to increase until the rats displayed a dislike for the cocaine. This caused them to consume less of it. As the levels of microRNA-212 decreased, cocaine consumption increased and the mice resembled human cocaine addicts in their desire to obtain more.[15]

It appears from these results that microRNA-212 is very important in regulating cocaine intake in rats and may very well do the same in humans. This is because microRNA-212 is also found in the human brain in an area known as the dorsal striatum, which has been linked to drug abuse and habit formation.

Paul J. Kenny, the senior author of the study, was very encouraged by the results. He stated, "The results of this study offer promise for the development of a totally new class of anti-addiction medications. Because we are beginning to map out how this specific microRNA works, we may be able to develop new compounds to manipulate the levels of microRNA-212 therapeutically with exquisite specificity, opening the possibility of new treatments for drug addiction."[16]

SUMMARY

Cocaine and crack addiction is a major societal and health problem. Many addicts have no intention of giving up their habit and attempting to straighten out their lives. Others sincerely want to break their addiction habit but, no matter how hard they try, they keep slipping back into addiction. Still others actually do succeed in beating their addiction to cocaine and crack and return to a normal, productive life. The reasons for these differences are many and very complex. Nevertheless, it is generally agreed that humanity would be much better off without these drugs.

Researchers all over the world are working to find cures for addiction to cocaine and crack and to develop a vaccine that will prohibit the body from becoming addicted to these susbstances. There have been enough encouraging results associated with research and therapeutic techniques to believe that, in time, there is a good chance that the scientists will succeed in helping those already addicted and in providing a vaccine to keep more people from becoming addicts.

Appendix: Classification of Controlled Substances

Formal Scheduling of Controlled Substances

Schedule I—(1) The drug or other substance has a high potential for abuse. (2) The drug or other substance has no currently accepted medical use in treatment in the United States. (3) There is a lack of accepted safety for use of the drug or other substance under medical supervision. (4) Examples of Schedule I substances include heroin, lysergic acid diethylamide (LSD), marijuana, and methaqualone.

Schedule II—(1) The drug or other substance has a high potential for abuse. (2) The drug or other substance has a currently accepted medical use in treatment in the United States or a currently accepted medical use with severe restrictions. (3) Abuse of the drug or other substance may lead to severe psychological or physical dependence. (4) Examples of Schedule II substances include morphine, phency-clidine (PCP), cocaine, methadone, and methamphetamine.

Schedule III—(1) The drug or other substance has less potential for abuse than the drugs or other substances in schedules I and II. (2) The drug or other substance has a currently accepted medical use in treatment in the United States. (3) Abuse of the drug or other substance may lead to moderate or low physical dependence or high psychological dependence. (4) Anabolic steroids, codeine and hydro-codone with aspirin or Tylenol, and some barbiturates are examples of Schedule III substances.

Schedule IV—(1) The drug or other substance has a low potential for abuse relative to the drugs or other substances in Schedule III. (2) The drug or other substance has a currently accepted medical use in treatment in the United States. (3) Abuse of the drug or other substance may lead to limited physical dependence or psychological dependence relative to the drugs or other substances in Schedule III. (4) Examples of drugs included in schedule IV are Darvon, Talwin, Equanil, Valium, and Xanax.

Schedule V—(1) The drug or other substance has a low potential for abuse relative to the drugs or other substances in Schedule IV. (2) The drug or other substance has a currently accepted medical use in treatment in the United States. (3) Abuse of the drug or other substances may lead to limited physical dependence or psychological dependence relative to the drugs or other substances in Schedule IV. (4) Cough medicines with codeine are examples of Schedule V drugs.

Source: U.S. Drug Enforcement Administration, "Chapter 1: The Controlled Substances Act," http://www.justice.gov/dea/pubs/abuse/1-csa.htm#Schedule%20I (accessed September 29, 2010).

Notes

Chapter 1

1. National Institute on Drug Abuse, "Cocaine: Abuse and Addiction," http://www.nida.nih.gov/researchreports/cocaine/whatis.html (accessed October 1, 2010).

2. Substance Abuse and Mental Health Services Administration, Office of Applied Studies, "*Results from the 2005 National Survey on Drug Use and Health: National findings* (NSDUH Series H-30, DHHS Publication No. SMA 06-4194)," Rockville, MD, tables G.3, G.28. 2006.

3. Wendy Moelker, "Cocaine Addiction: Effects of Smoking Cocaine," *Web4health*, July 22, 2008. http://web4health.info/en/answers/add-cocaine-damage.htm (accessed March 23, 2010).

4. S. Hayes, T. Moyer, D. Morley, and A. Bove, "Intravenous Cocaine Causes Epicardial Coronary Vasoconstriction in the Intact Dog," *American Heart Journal*, Volume 121, Issue 6, (June 1991), pp. 1639–1648, http://linkinghub.elsevier.com/retrieve/pii/0002870391900075 (accessed March 25, 2010).

5. DrugWarFacts.org, "Get the Facts: Drug Use Estimates," http://www.drugwarfacts.org/cms/Drug_Usage (accessed October 12, 2010).

6. Substance Abuse and Mental Health Services Administration, Office of Applied Studies, "*Results from the 2005 National Survey on Drug Use and Health: National findings* (NSDUH Series H-30, DHHS Publication No. SMA 06-4194)," Rockville, MD, tables G.3, G.28. 2006.

7. Ibid.

Chapter 2

1. Robert C. Petersen and Richard C. Stillman, "Cocaine: 1977," *National Institute on Drug Abuse Research Monograph Series #13*.

2. James A. Inciardi, "The War on Drugs II" (Palo Alto, Calif.: Mayfield Publishing Co., 1992), 6.

3. Albert Niemann, "Ueber Eine Neue Organische Base in den

Cocablättern" (On a New Organic Base in the Coca Leaves), *Archiv der Pharmazie,* Volume 153, 2 (1860): 129–256.

4. Andrew J. Humphrey and David O'Hagan, "Tropane Alkaloid Biosynthesis: A Century Old Problem Unresolved," *Natural Product Reports,* Volume 18, 5 (2001): 494–502, http://www.rsc.org/ej/NP/2001/b001713m.pdf (accessed April 8, 2010).

5. Brent Staples, "Coke Wars," *The New York Times,* February 6, 1994, http://www.nytimes.com/1994/02/06/books/coke-wars.html?pagewanted=1 (accessed on April 8, 2010).

6. William Barlow, *Looking Up at Down: The Emergence of Blues Culture,* (Philadelphia: Temple University Press, 1989), 207.

7. Bernardo Alexander Attias, "Cocaine/Crack," St. James Encyclopedia of Pop Culture, January 29, 2002. http://findarticles.com/p/articles/mi_g1epc/is_tov/ai_2419100264/?tag=content;col1 (accessed April 10, 2010).

8. Schaffer Library of Drug Policy, "Harrison Narcotics Tax Act, 1914," http://www.druglibrary.org/schaffer/History/e1910/harrisonact.htm (accessed April 10, 2010).

9. WGBH Boston, *Frontline: The Opium Kings,* http://www.pbs.org/wgbh/pages/frontline/shows/heroin/etc/history.html (accessed April 10, 2010).

10. Jeremy Hsu, "Majority of U.S. Cocaine Supply Cut with Veterinary Deworming Drug," *POPSCI,* December 18, 2009, http://www.popsci.com/science/article/2009-12/majority-us-cocaine-supply-cut-veterinary-deworming-drug (accessed April 12, 2010).

11. European Monitoring Centre for Drugs and Drug Addiction, "Purity of Cocaine Products at Retail Level, 2007," *EMCDDA,* July 1, 2009. http://www.emcdda.europa.eu/stats09/ppptab7a (accessed April 12, 2010).

12. Craig Reinarman and Harry G. Levine, *"Crack in America: Demon Drugs and Social Justice"* (Berkeley: University of California Press, 1997), 388.

13. Criminal Justice Policy Foundation, "Crack Facts," 2006, http://www.crack-facts.org/historyofcrack.html (accessed April 12, 2010).

14. U.S. Department of Justice, "The Anti-Drug Abuse Act of 1988," *Criminal Resource Manual,* http://www.justice.gov/usao/eousa/foia_reading

_room/usam/title9/crm00068
.htm (accessed April 13, 2010).

15. *San Jose Mercury News,*
"Criminal Docket for Case
#: 92-CR-551-ALL: USA v.
Blandon et al," May 11, 1995,
http://www.narconews.com/
darkalliance/drugs/library/13
.htm (accessed April 16, 2010).

Chapter 3

1. Eric H. Chudler, "Brain Facts
and Figures," University of
Washington, Seattle, http://
faculty.washington.edu/
chudler/facts.html (accessed
April 22, 2010).

2. D. Engblom et al., "Glutamate
Receptors on Dopamine Neurons Control the Persistence of
Cocaine Seeking," *Neuron,* Volume 59, 3 (August 14, 2008):
497–508, http://www.science-
direct.com/science?_ob=
ArticleURL&_udi=B6WSS-
4T6MHFJ-K&_user=10&_
coverDate=08%2F14%2F2008
&_rdoc=1&_fmt=high&_orig=
search&_sort=d&_docanchor
=&view=c&_acct=C000050221
&_version=1&_urlVersion=
0&_userid=10&md5=ef3b6b5
f200e4e1549d6df1b2252c377
(accessed April 25, 2010).

3. N. Uchimura and R.A. North,
"Actions of Cocaine on Rat
Nucleus Accumbens Neurons
In Vitro," *British Journal of*

Pharmacology, 99, 4 (April
1990), http://www.ncbi
.nlm.nih.gov/pmc/articles/
PMC1917561/ (accessed April
26, 2010).

4. W.K. Park et al., "Cocaine
Administered into the Medial
Prefrontal Cortex Reinstates
Cocaine-Seeking Behav-
ior by Increasing AMPA
Receptor-Mediated Gluta-
mate Transmission in the
Nucleus Accumbens," *The
Journal of Neuroscience,*
Volume 22, 7 (April 1, 2002):
http://www.jneurosci.org/cgi/
reprint/22/7/2916 (accessed
April 26, 2010).

5. Global Oneness, "Cocaine:
Encyclopedia II-Cocaine-
Pharmacology," http://www
.experiencefestival.com/a/
Cocaine_-_Pharmacology/
id/4952761 (accessed April 26,
2010).

6. Lynn Barkley Burnett, Carlos
J. Roldan, and Jonathan Adler,
"Toxicity, Cocaine," *emedicine,* March 19, 2010, http://
emedicine.medscape.com/
article/813959-overview
(accessed April 26, 2010).

7. Ibid.

Chapter 4

1. Basics, "Cocaine," http://www
.basics-network.org/virtualib/

data/Dropin_Cocaina_en.pdf (accessed May 3, 2010).

2. The Canyon, "The Three Stages of Drug Addiction," The Canyon Rehabilitation and Substance Abuse Treatment Center, http://www.thecyn .com/drug-addiction/the-three-stage-of-drug-addiction.html (accessed May 9, 2010).

3. Behave Net, Clinical Capsule, "Substance Dependence," http://www.behavenet.com/ capsules/disorders/subdep.htm (accessed May 9, 2010).

4. George Koob and Mary Jeanne Kreek, "Stress, Dysregulation of Drug Reward Pathways, and the Transition to Drug Dependence," *American Journal of Psychiatry*, 164, no. 8 (August 2007): 1149–1159, http://ajp .psychiatryonline.org/cgi/ content/full/164/8/l149 (accessed on January 11, 2011).

5. U.S. Drug Enforcement Administration, "Stimulants: Cocaine," http://www.justice. gov/dea/pubs/abuse/5-stim .htm (accessed May 8, 2010).

6. R. L. Hubbard et al., "Overview of 1-year Followup Outcomes in the Drug Abuse Treatment Outcome Study (DATOS)," *Psychology of Addictive Behaviors*, Volume 11, 4 (1997): 261–278.

7. J.C. Barden, "Crack Smoking Seen as a Peril to Lungs," *The New York Times*, December 24, 1989, http://www.nytimes .com/1989/12/24/us/crack-smoking-seen-as-a-peril-to-lungs.html (accessed May 11, 2010).

8. U.S. Drug Enforcement Administration, "Cocaine," http://www.justice.gov/ dea/concern/cocaine.html (accessed May 11, 2010).

9. Crack Facts, "STDs and Crack," http://www.crack-facts.org/ stdsandcrack.html (accessed October 13, 2010).

10. Susan Okie, "The Epidemic That Wasn't," *The New York Times*, January 26, 2009. http:// www.nytimes.com/2009/01/27/ health/27coca.html (accessed October 14, 2010).

11. Ibid.

12. Ibid.

13. Ibid.

14. Ibid.

15. Alan I. Leshner, "Statement on Children's Health Issues appearing before the Subcommittee on Labor, Health and Human Services, and Education Committee on Appropriations, United States House of Representatives," National Institute on Drug Abuse, October 29, 1997, http://archives .drugabuse.gov/Testimony/10–29-97Testimony.html (accessed May 11, 2010).

16. The March of Dimes, "Illicit Drug Use During Pregnancy," January 2008, http://www .marchofdimes.com/ professionals/14332_1169.asp (accessed May 11, 2010).

Chapter 5

1. Crimescreen.com, "Substance Abuse Statistics Every Employer Should Know." http://www.crimescreen.com/ stats.htm (accessed May 18, 2010).
2. Friends of NIDA, "Transition Paper to President Obama," October 2008, http://www .cpdd.vcu.edu/Pages/Index/ Index_PDFs/Transition PaperOctober20081.pdf.
3. Vivian Hope et al., "Frequency, Factors and Costs Associated with Injection Site Infections: Findings from a National Multi-site Survey of Injecting Drug Users in England," *BMC Infectious Diseases*, Volume 8, 120 (September 18, 2008), http:// ukpmc.ac.uk/articlerender .cgi?accid=PMC2600824 (accessed May 25, 2010).
4. Elisa Lloyd-Smith et al., "Prevalence and Correlates of Abscesses Among a Cohort of Injection Drug Users," *Harm Reduction Journal*, Volume 2, 24 (November 10, 2005), http://

pubmedcentralcanada .ca/articlerender.cgi?tool=pu bmed&pubmedid=16281979 (accessed May 25, 2010).
5. Janine Hutson, "A Prenatal Perspective on the Cost of Substance Abuse in Canada," *Journal of Fetal Alcohol Syndrome International*, Volume 4, e9 (May 30, 2006), http:// www.motherisk.org/JFAS_ documents/jfas_6006_e9.pdf (accessed May 25, 2010).
6. B. M. Lester, L.L. La Gasse, and R. Seifer, "Cocaine Exposure and Children: The Meaning of Subtle Effects," *Science*, Volume 282, 5389 (October 23, 1998), 633–634.
7. Matthew Hickley, "£833,000: The Real Cost to the Nation of a Drug Addict Revealed," *MailOnline*, June 14, 2008, http://www.dailymail.co.uk/ health/article-1026375/833- 000-The-real-cost-nation- drug-addict-revealed.html (accessed May 26, 2010).
8. National Institute on Drug Addiction, "NIDA Info Facts: Treatments for Drug Addiction," September 2009, http:// www.nida.nih.gov/infofacts/ treatmeth.html (accessed October 14, 2010).
9. Ibid.
10. Drug-Rehabs, "Cocaine Addiction Treatment," http://www

.drug-rehabs.com/cocaine-rehab.htm (accessed October 14, 2010).

11. CocaineEffects, "CocaineTreatment," http://www.cocaine-effects.com/cocaine-treatment.htm (accessed October 14, 2010).

12. Substance Abuse and Mental Health Services Administration (SAMHSA), "Substance Abuse Treatment Facility Locator," http://dasis3.samhsa.gov/ (accessed October 14, 2010).

13. Substance Abuse and Mental Health Services Administration (SAMHSA), "Substance Abuse Treatment Facility Locator: State Substance Abuse Agencies," http://findtreatment.samhsa.gov/ufds/abusedirectors (accessed October 15, 2010).

14. Cocaine Addiction Treatment, http://www.cocaineaddiction treatment.org/ (accessed October 15, 2010).

15. Drug Rehabs.Org, "Drug Rehab and Alcohol Addiction Treatment Information," http://www.drug-rehabs.org/ (accessed October 15, 2010).

Chapter 6

1. Eileen Ribeiro, *Dress and Morality,* (Gordonsville, Va.: Berg Publishers, 2003), 12–16.

2. Edward Huntington Williams, "Negro Cocaine 'Fiends' New Southern Menace," *The New York Times,* February 8, 1914, http://query.nytimes.com/gst/abstract.html?res=F60B14F7345F13738DDDA10894DA405B848DF1D3&scp=1&sq=NEGRO%20COCAINE%20%22FIENDS%22%20NEW%20SOUTHERN%20MENACE&st=cse (accessed October 18, 2010).

3. Edward Marshall, "Unlce Sam Is the Worst Drug Fiend in the World," *The New York Times,* March 12, 1911. http://query.nytimes.com/gst/abstract.html?res=F60C15F6385517738DDDAB0994DB405B818DF1D3&scp=1&sq=Unlce%20Sam%20is%20the%20Worst%20Drug%20Fiend%20in%20the%20World&st=cse (accessed October 18, 2010).

4. Williams, "Negro Cocaine 'Fiends.'"

5. Ibid.

6. "Harrison Narcotics Tax Act, 1914," *Schaffer Library of Drug Policy,* http://www.druglibrary.org/schaffer/history/e1910/harrisonact.htm (accessed June 29, 2010).

7. United States Drug Enforcement Administration, "Title 21-Food And Drugs, Chapter 13-Drug Abuse Prevention and Control, Subchapter 1-Control and Enforcement,

Section 801," http://www
.justice.gov/dea/pubs/csa.html
(accessed June 29, 2010).

8. Office of National Drug Control Policy, "Crack Facts and
Figures," http://www.white
housedrugpolicy.gov/drugfact/
crack/crack_ff.html#legislation
(accessed June 29, 2010).

9. "Arrested for Crack Cocaine:
Differences in Penal-
ties," Got Trouble, http://
guides.gottrouble.com/
Arrested_For_Crack_Cocaine_
%E2%80%93_Differences_
In_Penalties-a1196339.html
(accessed July 1, 2010).

10. Ibid.

11. U.S. Department of Justice,
"Drug Availability in the United
States," http://www.justice.gov/
ndic/pubs38/38661/cocaine.
htm (accessed July 1, 2010).

12. "Arrested for Crack Cocaine,"
Got Trouble.

Chapter 7

1. Kamika Dunlap, "Congress
Weighs Crack and Powder
Cocaine Sentencing," *Findlaw Blotter,* March 5, 2010.
http://blogs.findlaw.com/
blotter/2010/03/congress-
weighs-crack-and-powder-
cocaine-sentencing.html
(accessed July 11, 2010).

2. "H.R. 3245, The Fairness in
Cocaine Sentencing Act of
2009," Washingtonwatch.com,
http://www.washingtonwatch
.com/bills/show/111_HR_3245
.html#toc0 (accessed July 11,
2010).

3. *The Washington Post,* "The
Fair Sentencing Act Corrects a
Long-time Wrong in Cocaine
Cases," August 3, 2010, http://
www.washingtonpost
.com/wpdyn/ content/
article/2010/08/02/
AR2010080204360.html
(accessed January 18, 2011);
J. Lee, "President Obama
Signs the Fair Sentencing
Act," The White House Blog,
http://www.whitehouse.gov/
blog/2010/08/03/president-
obama-signs-fair-sentencing-
act (accessed January 18, 2011).

4. Larry Margasak, "Obama
Crack Sentencing Laws
Change in Works," *The Huff-
ington Post,* April 29, 2009,
http://www.huffingtonpost.
com/2009/04/29/obama-crack-
sentencing-la_n_192799.html
(accessed July 11, 2010).

5. "Senate OKs Change in Crack-
cocaine Laws," *Arizona Daily
Star,* March 18, 2010. http://
azstarnet.com/news/national/
article_6beca5c3-c29a-5caa-
baed-cd0131ec3c48.html
(accessed July 11, 2010).

6. "Brain Imaging Study of the
Effects of Modafinil in Cocaine

Addiction," Assistance Publique, Hôpitaux de Paris, http://clinicaltrials.gov/ct2/show/NCT00701532?term=cocaine+addiction&rank=1 (accessed July 12, 2010).

7. "Citicoline for Bipolar I Disorder and Cocaine Dependence," University of Texas Southwestern Medical Center, http://clinicaltrials.gov/ct2/show/NCT00619723?term=cocaine+addiction&rank=6 (accessed July 13, 2010).

8. "Clinical Trial of Topiramate for Cocaine Addiction," Johns Hopkins University, http://clinicaltrials.gov/ct2/show/NCT00685178?term=cocaine+addiction&rank=11 (accessed July 13, 2010).

9. "Cognitive Enhancement and Relapse Prevention in Cocaine Addiction," University of Arkansas, http://clinicaltrials.gov/ct2/show/NCT01067846?term=cocaine+addiction&rank=23 (accessed July 13, 2010).

10. "A Contribution to the Analysis of Phenotypic Heterogeneity in Crack/Cocaine Addiction: a Case Control Study," Centre Hospitalier Universitaire de Fort-de-France, Martinique, http://clinicaltrials.gov/ct2/show/NCT01025219?term=crack+addiction&rank=1 (accessed July 13, 2010).

11. "Cocaine Vaccine Shows Promise for Treating Addiction," National Institute on Drug Abuse, October 5, 2009, http://www.drugabuse.gov/newsroom/09/NR10–05.html (accessed July 13, 2010).

12. Ibid.

13. Rachel Saslow, "Testing of Cocaine Vaccine Shows It Does Not Fully Blunt Cravings for the Drug," *The Washington Post,* January 5, 2010, http://www.washingtonpost.com/wp-dyn/content/article/2010/01/04/AR2010010402752.html (accessed July 13, 2010).

14. "NIH-Supported Finding on Cocaine Addiction: Tiny Molecule, Big Promise," National Institute on Drug Abuse, July 7, 2010, http://drugabuse.gov/newsroom/10/NR7-07.html (accessed July 14, 2010).

15. Ibid.

16. Ibid.

Glossary

abscess   A collection of pus in tissues that is usually caused by a localized bacterial infection.

acetylcholine   A neurotransmitter found in several areas of the body and the brain that is involved in transmission of nerve impulses.

acetylcholinesterase   An enzyme that breaks down the neurotransmitter acetylcholine when it is no longer needed in a synapse.

adrenergic crisis   A sudden dramatic increase in the levels of epinephrine and norepinephrine that brings about extreme elevation of blood pressure and heart rate that may be life threatening. The leading cause in the United States is cocaine overdose.

alpha-methyldopa   A psychoactive drug used to treat high blood pressure (hypertension).

anhedonia   The inability to experience pleasure.

anti-inflammatory drugs   Drugs that reduce inflammation directly but do not affect the nervous system.

benzoylmethylecgonine   The chemical name for cocaine.

black market   The dealing of goods and services that are not part of the official economy of a country. It usually involves illegal products such as drugs, stolen vehicles, and prostitution.

blood-brain barrier   A protective structure consisting of endothelial cells tightly packed together that line the capillaries of the brain. It is designed to protect the brain from toxic substances in the bloodstream by not allowing them to pass from the blood into the brain.

cardiac arrest   The abrupt stopping of the heart.

cellulitis   Inflammation of connective or subcutaneous tissue.

central nervous system   The part of the nervous system that consists of the brain and spinal cord only.

chronicus   Latin word meaning "of time" from which the English word *chronic* is derived.

cocaethylene   A chemical that is structurally similar to cocaine that is formed when cocaine and ethyl alcohol are ingested simultaneously.

cocaine base   The form of cocaine produced in the second step of processing. Coca paste is made from dried coca leaves after which cocaine base is extracted. The base is further processed into pure cocaine hydrochloride powder.

cocaine bugs   The hallucinatory sensation caused by cocaine use that bugs are crawling under the skin.

cocaine hydrochloride   The powder of cocaine.

coca plant   A plant that is native to northwestern South America from which cocaine is extracted.

coke bugs   *See* cocaine bugs.

corpus callosum   A structure made of nerves in the center of the brain that connects the left and right hemispheres of the cerebrum.

cortex   The outer portion of the brain, made of nerve cell bodies.

corticosteroids   Steroid hormones produced in the adrenal cortex that are involved in several bodily processes, including the stress and immune responses and regulation of inflammation.

crack   Pellet-sized pieces of highly purified cocaine that are smoked to achieve a quick high.

crack baby   A physiologically addicted baby born to a mother who used crack while pregnant.

crack lip   Blistered and cracked lips that develop as a result of pressing a very hot pipe to the lips while smoking crack.

crack lung   Scarring and permanent damage of the lungs due to excessive smoking of crack cocaine.

craving   An intense desire to obtain and use a drug such as cocaine or crack that develops when a user attempts to stop using or between uses.

delusional parasitosis   A form of psychosis in which individuals falsely believe that they are infested with parasites. It is the technical term for crack bugs.

dopamine   A neurotransmitter found in the central nervous system that is associated with feelings of ecstasy.

drug addiction   The psychological and physiological compulsion to obtain and use a drug such as cocaine or crack.

endothelial cells   A single layer of tightly packed, smooth, thin cells that lines the inner surface of the blood vessels that nourish the brain. They form the blood-brain barrier.

erythoxyline   The original name for cocaine, given to it by its discoverer, Friedrich Gaedcke, in 1855.

ethylbenzoylecgonine   *See* cocaethylene.

extinction   In behaviorism, the loss of a conditioned response due to the absence of reinforcement.

formic acid   The simplest organic acid, which occurs naturally in the poison of ants and in the plant known as the stinging nettle.

formication   *See* cocaine bugs.

freebase cocaine   Cocaine in its pure, basic form.

freebasing   The process of purifying cocaine by dissolving it in sodium hydroxide, ether, or other substances and then filtering off the precipitate.

gangrene   The process whereby tissue dies due to obstruction of blood flow thus stopping the supply of oxygen.

glutamate   A form of the amino acid glutamic acid that acts as a neurotransmitter.

hydrophobic   Referring to molecules that are repelled by water, such as lipid compounds. The literal translation of the word is "water fearing."

insufflation   Inhaling a powdered drug into the nasal cavity. Also referred to as snorting.

khronikos   Greek word meaning "of time" from which the English word *chronic* is derived.

levamisole   A drug used to treat infestations with worms that is also used to "cut" cocaine.

limbic system   A group of interconnected structures in the brain that act as the seat of emotion, motivation, and behavior.

methadone   A synthetic narcotic, similar to morphine, used to substitute for heroin in users addicted to it.

monoamine oxidase inhibitors Drugs that inhibit the activity of the enzyme monoamine oxidase. This enzyme is used to break down monoamine neurotransmitters such as norepinephrine and serotonin.

myelin A soft, white, fatty substance that insulates the axons of most nerves in the central and peripheral nervous systems.

narcolepsy A condition that causes an individual to experience frequent, uncontrolled periods of deep sleep.

nasal septum The bony and cartilaginous wall that separates the nasal cavity (nose) into two halves.

necrotic Describing tissue that is dead as a result of injury or disease.

neuroendocrine system The term used to describe the close relationship between the nervous system and the endocrine system.

neurotransmitters Chemicals that are secreted into a synapse to allow transmission of a nerve impulse.

norepinephrine A neurotransmitter released in the central and autonomic nervous systems that brings about vasoconstriction, elevated blood pressure, and several other responses.

nucleus accumbens A collection of neurons in the brain that are an integral part of the feelings associated with rewards, pleasure, and addiction.

organophosphates Organic compounds that contain phosphorus that has strong neurotoxic properties. Chemicals of this class were originally used as nerve gas and are now used in insecticides.

paranoia A psychiatric disorder characterized by the delusion that the individual is being persecuted or stalked by others.

peripheral nervous system The nervous system of the body that does not include the brain and spinal cord.

phenytoin An anticonvulsant drug used to treat grand mal seizures of epilepsy.

physical dependence A condition that develops from chronic drug use wherein tolerance to the drug develops so that if the drug is withdrawn abruptly, serious symptoms result.

postsynaptic neuron The nerve that is located after a synapse. This is the nerve that receives the impulse from the presynaptic neuron.

prefrontal cortex The gray matter of the anterior portion of the frontal lobe of the brain, responsible for much behavioral and emotional functioning.

presynaptic neuron The nerve that is located before the synapse. This nerve sends the impulse to the postsynaptic neuron.

pseudocholinesterase An enzyme that is slightly different from acetylcholinesterase. Instead of breaking down acetylcholine, this enzyme breaks down butyrylcholine, a synthetic compound used for chemical analyses.

reserpine A drug obtained from the plant *Rauwolfia serpentina,* used to treat hypertension.

respiratory arrest The cessation of breathing often associated with a heart attack or a neurological abnormality.

reuptake transporters Proteins designed to facilitate the reabsorption of a neurotransmitter into the presynaptic neuron from where it came.

RNA Ribonucleic acid, the single-stranded molecule of genetic material transcribed from the DNA molecule and used in the process of protein synthesis.

seizure A sudden convulsion as in an epileptic attack.

serotonin A monoamine stimulatory neurotransmitter found in the brain and gastric mucosa.

snorting *See* insufflation.

speedball A combination of a stimulant and a depressant, such as cocaine and heroin.

substance dependence A diagnosis made when an individual continues to use drugs or alcohol despite problems relating to their use.

synapse The junctional space between two nerves or a nerve and a muscle motor end plate where a neurotransmitter is needed to propagate a nerve impulse.

tachycardia A heart rate of greater than 100 beats per minute in an adult who is not exercising.

tachyphylaxis A decreased response to a drug taken over time so that continually larger doses are required to achieve the same effect.

tricyclic antidepressants Antidepressant drugs whose basic structure contains three rings of atoms.

tropane An amine from which cocaine, atropine, and other alkaloids are derived.

tropinone A synthetic precursor to atropine, first synthesized in 1917, that shares the same tropane core structure with cocaine.

ventral tegmental area A group of neurons on the floor of the midbrain that secretes dopamine and is involved in the reward and addiction circuits of the brain.

Vin Mariani A tonic created in 1863 by Angelo Mariani made from Bordeaux wine and coca leaves.

withdrawal Discontinuing the use of an addictive drug. Specific symptoms are associated with withdrawal that are dependent on which drug was being used.

further Resources

Books and Articles

"Crack vs. Powder Cocaine: A Gulf in Penalties." *U.S. News Politics & Policy,* October 1, 2007. http://politics.usnews.com/news/national/articles/2007/10/01/crack-vs-powder-cocaine-a-gulf-in-penalties.html.

Emery, Theo. "Will Crack-Cocaine Sentencing Reform Help Current Cons?" *Time,* August 7, 2009. http://www.time.com/time/nation/article/0,8599,1915131,00.html.

Feiling, Tom. *The Candy Machine: How Cocaine Took Over the World.* London: Penguin Books, 2009.

———. *Cocaine Nation: How the White Trade Took Over the World.* Trenton, Tex.: Pegasus Publishing, 2010.

Gootenberg, Paul. *Andean Cocaine: The Making of a Global Drug.* Chapel Hill: The University of North Carolina Press, 2008.

Henderson, Elizabeth Connell. *Understanding Addiction.* Jackson: University Press of Mississippi, 2000.

Karch, Steven B. *A Brief History of Cocaine.* Boca Raton, Fla.: CRC Press, 2006.

MacGregor, Felipe E. (ed). *Coca and Cocaine: An Andean Perspective.* Westport, Conn.: Greenwood Press, 1993.

Marcy, William L. *The Politics of Cocaine: How U.S. Foreign Policy Has Created a Thriving Drug Industry in Central and South America.* Chicago: Lawrence Hill Books, 2010.

Ottomanelli, Gennaro. *Children and Addiction.* Westport, Conn.: Praeger Publishers, 1995.

Ricks, Joel. *Crack Cocaine: The Enemy of This Age.* Bloomington, Ind.: Xlibris, 2009.

Roleff, Tamara L. *Compact Research, Cocaine and Crack.* San Diego: Reference Point Press, 2008.

Tervalon, Jervey, and Gary Phillips (eds.). *The Cocaine Chronicles.* New York: Akashic Books, 2005.

Webb, Gary. *Dark Alliance: The CIA, the Contras, and the Crack Cocaine Explosion.* Toronto: Hushion House, 1999.

Web Sites

Center for Substance Abuse Research, University of Maryland: Crack Cocaine
http://www.cesar.umd.edu/cesar/drugs/crack.asp

Cocaine Effects
http://www.cocaine-effects.com

EMedicinehealth: Cocaine Abuse
http://www.emedicinehealth.com/cocaine_abuse/article_em.htm

In Search of the Big Bang: What Is Crack Cocaine?
http://www.cocaine.org

Interpol: Cocaine
http://www.interpol.int/public/Drugs/cocaine/default.asp

MedicineNet.com: Cocaine and Crack Abuse
http://www.medicinenet.com/cocaine_and_crack_abuse/article .htm

National Drug Intelligence Center, U.S. Department of Justice: Crack Cocaine Fast Facts
http://www.justice.gov/ndic/pubs3/3978/index.htm

National Institute on Drug Abuse: Crack and Cocaine
http://www.nida.nih.gov/pdf/infofacts/cocaine07.pdf

National Institute on Drug Abuse: NIDA InfoFacts: Cocaine
http://www.drugabuse.gov/infofacts/cocaine.html

National Institute on Drug Abuse: Research Report Series, Cocaine: Abuse and Addiction
http://www.nida.nih.gov/researchreports/cocaine/cocaine.html

Office of National Drug Control Policy: Cocaine
http://www.whitehousedrugpolicy.gov/drugfact/cocaine/index .html

Office of National Drug Control Policy: Crack
http://www.whitehousedrugpolicy.gov/drugfact/crack/index.html

The Partnership at Drugfree.org: Cocaine/Crack
http://www.drugfree.org/portal/drug_guide/cocaine

Psychology Today: Cocaine
http://www.psychologytoday.com/conditions/cocaine

U.S. Drug Enforcement Administration: Cocaine
http://www.justice.gov/dea/concern/cocaine.html

U.S. National Library of Medicine: Cocaine
http://www.nlm.nih.gov/medlineplus/cocaine.html

WebMD: Cocaine Use and Its Effects
http://www.webmd.com/mental-health/cocaine-use-and-its-effects

Index

About the Author

Dr. Alan I. Hecht is a practicing chiropractor in New York. He is also an adjunct professor at Farmingdale State College and Nassau Community College and an adjunct associate professor at the C.W. Post campus of Long Island University. He teaches courses in medical microbiology, anatomy and physiology, comparative anatomy, human physiology, embryology, and general biology. In addition, he is the course coordinator for Human Biology at Hofstra University where he is an adjunct assistant professor.

Dr. Hecht received his B.S. in Biology-Pre-Medical Studies from Fairleigh Dickinson University in Teaneck, New Jersey. He received his M.S. in Basic Medical Sciences from the New York University School of Medicine. He also received his Doctor of Chiropractic (D.C.) degree from New York Chiropractic College in Brookville, New York.

About the Consulting Editor

Consulting editor **David J. Triggle, Ph.D.,** is a SUNY Distinguished Professor and the University Professor at the State University of New York at Buffalo. These are the two highest academic ranks of the university. Professor Triggle received his education in the United Kingdom with a Ph.D. degree in chemistry at the University of Hull. Following post-doctoral fellowships at the University of Ottawa (Canada) and the University of London (United Kingdom) he assumed a position in the School of Pharmacy at the University at Buffalo. He served as chairman of the Department of Biochemical Pharmacology from 1971 to 1985 and as Dean of the School of Pharmacy from 1985 to 1995. From 1996 to 2001 he served as Dean of the Graduate School and from 1999 to 2001 was also the University Provost. He is currently the University Professor, in which capacity he teaches bioethics and science policy, and is President of the Center for Inquiry Institute, a think tank located in Amherst, New York and devoted to issues around the public understanding of science. In the latter respect he is a major contributor to the online M.Ed. program—"Science and The Public"—in the Graduate School of Education and The Center for Inquiry.